# PATHWAYS

## Reading, Writing, and Critical Thinking

## FOUNDATIONS

## Laurie Blass    Mari Vargo

NATIONAL GEOGRAPHIC LEARNING | HEINLE CENGAGE Learning

Australia • Brazil • Japan • Korea • Mexico • Singapore • Spain • United Kingdom • United States

KH

**Pathways Foundations**
**Reading, Writing, and Critical Thinking**
Laurie Blass and Mari Vargo

Publisher: Andrew Robinson

Executive Editor: Sean Bermingham

Development Editor: Charlotte Sharman

Contributing Editor: Sylvia Bloch

Director of Global Marketing: Ian Martin

Marketing Manager: Emily Stewart

Director of Content and Media Production:
  Michael Burggren

Senior Content Project Manager: Daisy Sosa

Manufacturing Buyer: Marybeth Hennebury

Cover Design: Page 2, LLC

Cover Image: Stephen Alvarez/
          National Geographic Stock

Interior Design: Page 2, LLC

Composition: Page 2, LLC

International Student Edition:

ISBN-13: 978-1-285-44212-9

U.S. Edition:

ISBN-13: 978-1-285-45057-5

**National Geographic Learning**
20 Channel Center Street
Boston, MA 02210
USA

Cengage Learning is a leading provider of customized learning solutions with office locations around the globe, including Singapore, the United Kingdom, Australia, Mexico, Brazil, and Japan. Locate your local office at: **ngl.cengage.com**

Cengage Learning products are represented in Canada by Nelson Education, Ltd.

Visit National Geographic Learning online at **ngl.cengage.com**
Visit our corporate website at **www.cengage.com**

Printed in the United States of America
1 2 3 4 5 6 7 8 15 14 13

11/12/13

1

2

3

4

5

6

7

8

# PLACES TO EXPLORE IN

▲ Mexico has perhaps
more circuses than
any other country.
**page 67**

▲ In 2007, pilot Barrington Irving
took off from Florida on a trip
around the world. **page 59**

▲ In Paris, users can pay to use cycles
at hundreds of docking stations
around the city. **page 49**

Madidi National Park in Bolivia is one of
the world's last great tropical rain forests.
**page 99**

# PATHWAYS

▲ The Libyan Desert is one of explorer Kira Salak's many challenging destinations. **page 30**

▲ 800 years ago, a man in southern Turkey invented a very special clock. **page115**

▲ Scientist Albert Lin is hoping to find the lost tomb of Genghis Khan in a remote part of Mongolia. **page 77**

The world's largest population of green sea turtles can be found off the coast of northern Australia. **page 96**

# Scope and Sequence

| Unit | Academic Pathways | Vocabulary |
|---|---|---|
|  **1** **Our World** *Page 1* **Academic Track:** Sociology/ Anthropology | **Lesson A:** Identifying purpose Reflecting **Lesson B:** Reading a summary with infographics **Lesson C:** Writing sentences about your life today | Using suffixes to make adverbs Applying vocabulary in a personalized context Identifying meaning from context **Word Usage:** *male* and *female* **Word Partners:** *common; habits* **Word Link:** *-ly* |
|  **2** **Risk Takers** *Page 19* **Academic Track:** Psychology/ Sociology | **Lesson A:** Previewing Analyzing sources **Lesson B:** Reading biographical profiles **Lesson C:** Writing sentences about risk taking | Identifying parts of speech Identifying meaning from context Applying vocabulary in a personalized context **Word Usage:** parts of speech **Word Partners:** *goal* |
|  **3** **On the Move** *Page 37* **Academic Track:** Interdisciplinary | **Lesson A:** Previewing Analyzing pros and cons **Lesson B:** Reading a passage with related infographics **Lesson C:** Writing comparative sentences about transportation | Differentiating adjectives and nouns Identifying meaning from context Applying vocabulary in a personalized context **Word Partners:** *public, lose, idea, spend* **Word Link:** *-ful* |
|  **4** **Following a Dream** *Page 55* **Academic Track:** Interdisciplinary | **Lesson A:** Understanding main ideas and supporting ideas Making inferences **Lesson B:** Reading a biographical narrative **Lesson C:** Writing sentences about the future | Identifying meaning from context Differentiating verbs and nouns Applying vocabulary in a personalized context **Word Partners:** *knowledge* **Word Usage:** *graduate* **Word Link:** noun endings |

| Reading | Writing | Viewing | Critical Thinking |
|---|---|---|---|
| Understanding infographics<br><br>Predicting<br><br>Understanding gist and main ideas<br><br>Identifying key details<br><br>**Skill Focus:**<br>Identifying purpose | **Goal:**<br>Writing sentences about your life today<br><br>**Language:**<br>What is a sentence?<br>Simple present tense of *be* and other verbs | **Video:**<br>*7 Billion*<br><br>Predicting<br>Viewing for key details<br>Synthesizing information | Guessing meaning from context<br>Synthesizing and Reflecting<br><br>**CT Focus:**<br>Reflecting |
| Understanding photo captions<br><br>Previewing and predicting<br><br>Understanding the gist<br><br>Identifying main ideas and key details<br><br>Synthesizing information from two readings<br><br>**Skill Focus:**<br>Previewing (I) | **Goal:**<br>Writing sentences about risk taking<br><br>**Language:**<br>Negative simple present of *be* and other verbs<br>Adverbs of frequency | **Video:**<br>*Killer Crocs*<br><br>Brainstorming ideas<br>Viewing for key details<br>Synthesizing information | Guessing meaning from context<br>Analyzing a text<br>Synthesizing/Making connections<br>Reflecting/Relating<br><br>**CT Focus:**<br>Analyzing sources |
| Understanding infographics<br><br>Previewing and predicting<br><br>Understanding the gist<br><br>Identifying key details<br><br>Summarizing using a concept map<br><br>**Skill Focus:**<br>Previewing (II) | **Goal:**<br>Writing comparative sentences about transportation<br><br>**Language:**<br>Comparatives<br>Using *because* | **Video:**<br>*Crossing America*<br><br>Making predictions<br>Viewing for key details<br>Sequencing and synthesizing information | Guessing meaning from context<br>Synthesizing information to make a decision<br>Analyzing pros and cons<br><br>**CT Focus:**<br>Analyzing pros and cons |
| Understanding survey information<br><br>Previewing and predicting<br><br>Understanding the gist<br><br>Understanding a sequence<br><br>Identifying key details<br><br>**Skill Focus:**<br>Understanding main and supporting ideas of paragraphs | **Goal:**<br>Writing sentences about the future<br><br>**Language:**<br>Using *plan*, *want*, and *hope*<br>Using time expressions | **Video:**<br>*Arctic Flyer*<br><br>Brainstorming ideas<br>Viewing for details<br>Synthesizing information | Making inferences<br>Synthesizing<br><br>**CT Focus:**<br>Making inferences |

# Scope and Sequence

| Unit | Academic Pathways | Vocabulary |
|------|-------------------|------------|

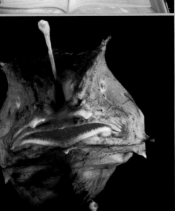

| Reading | Writing | Viewing | Critical Thinking |
|---|---|---|---|
| Interpreting maps and charts<br><br>Predicting<br>Understanding the gist<br>Identifying key details<br>Summarizing using a Venn diagram<br><br>**Skill Focus:**<br>Scanning for key details | **Goal:**<br>Writing sentences about information technology<br><br>**Language:**<br>Infinitives of purpose<br>Coordinating conjunctions: *and*, *but*, *or* | **Video:**<br>*Citizen Scientists*<br><br>Making predictions<br>Viewing for key details<br>Synthesizing information | Evaluating reasons<br>Synthesizing<br><br>**CT Focus:**<br>Inferring meaning from context |
| Understanding classifications<br><br>Previewing and predicting<br>Understanding main ideas<br>Identifying key details<br><br>**Skill Focus:**<br>Understanding reasons | **Goal:**<br>Writing sentences about endangered animals<br><br>**Language:**<br>Giving reasons<br>Speculating about the future | **Video:**<br>*Wonders of Madidi*<br><br>Brainstorming ideas<br>Viewing for key details<br>Synthesizing information | Relating information<br>Synthesizing<br><br>**CT Focus:**<br>Analyzing causes and effects |
| Interpreting text and visuals<br><br>Predicting<br>Understanding a process<br>Identifying key details<br>Completing a summary<br>Understanding supporting ideas<br><br>**Skill Focus:**<br>Understanding pronoun reference | **Goal:**<br>Writing sentences to support an argument<br><br>**Language:**<br>Simple past<br>Simple past of *be* | **Video:**<br>*The Golden Age*<br><br>Viewing for general understanding and specific information<br>Relating video content to a reading text | Guessing meaning from context<br>Synthesizing<br><br>**CT Focus:**<br>Analyzing an argument |
| Understanding infographics<br><br>Predicting<br>Identifying key details<br>Identifying problems and solutions<br>Completing an outline<br><br>**Skill Focus:**<br>Taking notes | **Goal:**<br>Writing sentences to express your opinion<br><br>**Language:**<br>Introducing your opinion<br>Using *should* | **Video:**<br>*Mapping the Labyrinth*<br><br>Making predictions<br>Viewing for general understanding<br>Synthesizing information | Evaluating relative importance<br>Guessing meaning from context<br><br>**CT Focus:**<br>Inferring and evaluating reasons |

## Each unit has three lessons.

Lessons A and B develop academic reading skills and vocabulary by focusing on two aspects of the unit theme. A video section acts as a content bridge between Lessons A and B. The language and content in these sections provide the stimulus for a final writing task (Lesson C).

The **unit theme** focuses on an academic content area relevant to students' lives, such as Sociology, Psychology, and Science and Technology.

## Academic Pathways

highlight the main academic skills of each lesson.

○ Following a Dream

UNIT 4

ACADEMIC PATHWAYS
Lesson A: Understanding main ideas and supporting ideas
Making inferences
Lesson B: Reading a biographical narrative
Lesson C: Writing sentences about the future

### Think and Discuss

1. What were some of your dreams for the future when you were a child? (For example, what job did you hope to have? What places did you want to visit?)
2. What are some of your dreams for the future now? Are they different?

▲ A team of explorers celebrates reaching the North Pole.

55

## *Exploring the Theme*

provides a visual introduction to the unit. Learners are encouraged to think critically and share ideas about the unit topic.

○ Exploring the Theme

Read the information and answer the questions.

1. What age group did Visa survey? What do those people dream of doing?
2. In the travel survey, which country did people from all regions plan to visit?
3. How do the survey results compare with your dreams and plans?

### Top Destinations

This chart shows the percentage of travelers from different regions who plan to visit certain countries in the next two years.

| People from . . . | Plan to visit . . . | |
|---|---|---|
| Asia Pacific | Japan | 30% |
| | United States | 21% |
| | United Kingdom | 20% |
| the Americas | United States | 34% |
| | United Kingdom | 26% |
| | Italy | 23% |
| Europe, Middle East, and Africa | Italy | 15% |
| | France, Spain | 14% |
| | United Kingdom | 13% |

Sources: www.visa.com.sg/aboutvisa/research/index.shtml
http://www.visa-asia.com/milionaire/

## Dreaming **Big**

Were you born between 1982 and 1995? If so, you are part of "Gen Y." These people make up more than 25 percent of the world's population.

What are the dreams of Gen Y? In 2011, the company Visa asked Gen Y people in different countries about their dreams for the future. The results showed that young people worldwide share many of the same dreams. For example, many Gen Y people dream of having their own business, exploring other cultures, and traveling.

In another survey, Visa asked 11,620 adults around the world about their travel plans for the next two years. One of the top travel choices in 2011 was the United Kingdom. People also planned to visit Japan, Australia, the United States, and China. Visa also asked people about their dream destinations—places they hope to visit one day in the future. Japan was the top choice (7 percent), above the United States, Maldives, Italy, France, and Australia (4 percent each).

56 | UNIT 4

FOLLOWING A DREAM | 57

In **Preparing to Read**, learners are introduced to key vocabulary items from the reading passage. Lessons A and B each present and practice ten target vocabulary items.

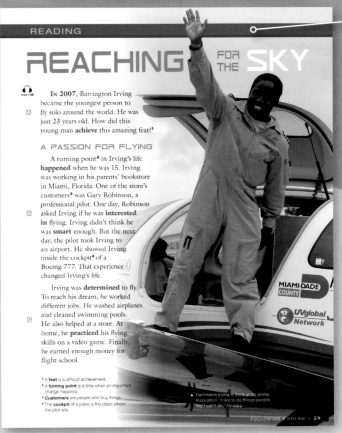

**Reading A** presents a text related to the unit theme. Each reading passage is recorded on the audio program.

**Viewing** tasks related to an authentic National Geographic video serve as a content bridge between Lessons A and B. (Video scripts are on pages 147–150.)

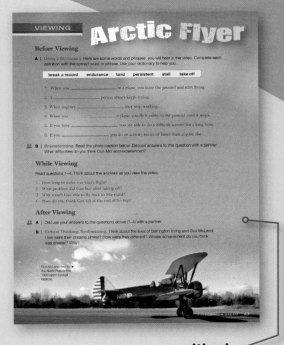

**Guided comprehension tasks and reading strategy instruction** enable learners to improve their academic literacy and critical thinking skills.

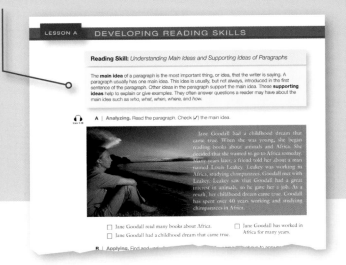

Learners need to use their **critical thinking skills** to relate video content to information in the previous reading.

### Vocabulary boxes

develop learners' awareness
of word structure, collocations,
and usage.

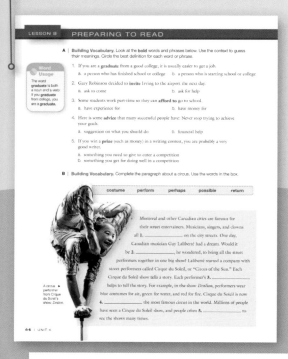

**LESSON B**    **READING**

# LIFE IN THE RING

**AS A CHILD,** Emily Ainsworth loved the colorful world of traveling circuses. As she grew older, she also became interested in other cultures. Above all, she wanted to travel. "England is a small country," she says. "I saved up for years . . . so that I could **afford to** fly abroad."

Ainsworth had many part-time jobs to pay for her travels, even working as a toilet cleaner. She also began to learn photography. When she was 16, she had enough money to travel to Mexico. The experience changed her life. She fell in love with Mexican culture and was determined to **return** one day.

As a 22-year-old anthropology **graduate**, Ainsworth got her chance. She won a BBC[1] contest called "Journey of a Lifetime." The **prize** of $4,000 went to the person with the most unusual adventure travel idea. Ainsworth's plan was to travel to Mexico to learn about the lives of circus workers. If **possible**, she wanted to become a circus worker herself.

Mexico has **perhaps** more circuses than any other country. One of the smaller, family-run circuses is the Circo Padilla. Soon after arriving in Mexico, Ainsworth met Padilla's ringmaster, Don Humberto. He **invited** her to visit his circus.

On her first day in Circo Padilla, one of the dancers could not **perform**. Don Humberto asked Ainsworth if she wanted to be a dancer. Five minutes later, Ainsworth says, she was in a dancer's **costume**. She stepped into the ring as "Princess Aurora." It was, she says, "like a childhood dream come true."

Emily Ainsworth took ▲
this photo of a young girl
looking up at performers
in one of Mexico's
traveling circuses.

**66** | UNIT 4

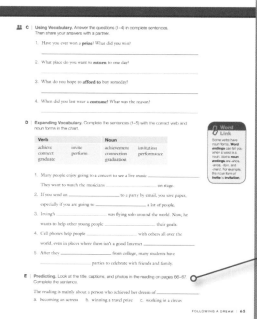

### Guided pre-reading tasks and strategy tips encourage

learners to think critically about what
they are going to read.

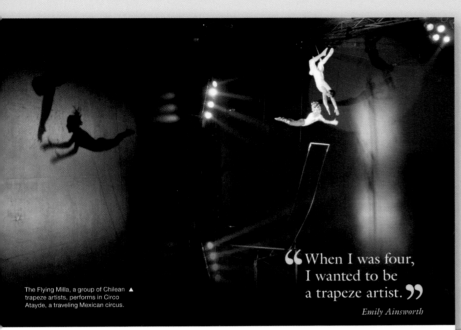

"When I was four, I wanted to be a trapeze artist."

*Emily Ainsworth*

The Flying Milla, a group of Chilean ▲
trapeze artists, performs in Circo
Atayde, a traveling Mexican circus.

F · As a dancing circus princess, Ainsworth performed and lived with the other circus workers. As an anthropologist[2] and photographer, she studied and took pictures of circus life. Most days passed in a "sleepy haze,"[3] she says. But at night, the circus world came alive.

G · Ainsworth now has a career as a journalist[4] and photographer. Wherever she travels, she still feels a deep connection with Mexico and returns there often. "I still feel like a part of that world," she says.

H · Her **advice** to young people is to hold on to their childhood dreams. "When you're eight years old," she says, "you know that anything is possible."

▲ Emily Ainsworth with a circus performer in Mexico.

[1] The **BBC** (British Broadcasting Corporation) is a British TV, radio, and news organization.
[2] An **anthropologist** studies people, societies, and cultures.
[3] If you are in **a sleepy haze**, you are not thinking clearly because you have not had enough sleep.
[4] A **journalist** writes for a newspaper, magazine, or other media.

FOLLOWING A DREAM | 67

---

LESSON B    UNDERSTANDING THE READING

**A | Understanding the Gist.** Look back at your answer for exercise **E** on page 65. Was your prediction correct?

**B | Identifying Main Ideas.** Write the letter of the correct paragraph (A, B, C, E, F) from the reading on pages 66–67 next to its main idea.

_____ 1. Ainsworth won some money, so she was able to return to Mexico.

_____ 2. Ainsworth performed in the circus while she studied it.

_____ 3. Ainsworth had two early dreams: traveling and working in a circus.

_____ 4. Ainsworth's first trip to Mexico changed her life.

_____ 5. Ainsworth got a job in the circus because one of the dancers could not perform.

**C | Understanding Supporting Ideas.** Complete the supporting ideas with details from the reading. Which main idea does each one support? Write the correct paragraph letter from exercise **B** next to each supporting idea.

| Supporting Idea | Paragraph |
|---|---|
| 1. To save money to go to Mexico the first time, Ainsworth _____ | ____ |
| 2. Ainsworth got money to go to Mexico again because she _____ | ____ |
| 3. When she was not performing, Ainsworth _____ | ____ |

**D | Critical Thinking: Making Inferences.** Discuss the questions (1–2) in a small group. Underline information on pages 66–67 that helps you answer each question.

1. How did Ainsworth feel about being a circus dancer?
2. How does Ainsworth feel about Mexico now?

**D | Critical Thinking: Synthesizing.** Discuss these questions in a small group.

1. In what ways are Barrington Irving and Emily Ainsworth similar?
2. Whose dream would you most like to follow? Why?

**Critical thinking tasks**
require learners to analyze, synthesize, and critically evaluate ideas and information in each reading.

▲ **Lesson B's reading passage**
presents a further aspect of the unit theme, using a variety of text types and graphic formats.

The **Goal of Lesson C** is for learners to relate their own views and experience to the theme of the unit by completing a guided writing assignment.

Integrated **grammar practice and writing skill development** provides scaffolding for the writing assignment.

The **Independent Student Handbook** provides further language support and self-study strategies for independent learning.

▶ see pages 151-156

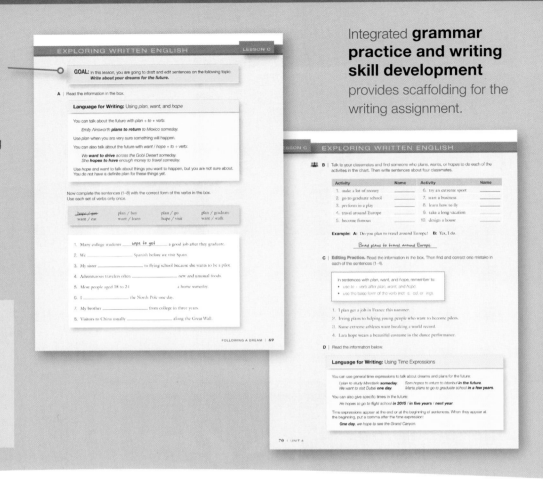

# Resources for *Pathways* Foundations

**Video DVD** with authentic National Geographic clips relating to each of the ten units.

**Teacher's Guide** including teacher's notes, expansion activities, rubrics for evaluating written assignments, and answer keys for activities in the Student Book.

**Audio CDs** with audio recordings of the Student Book reading passages.

A **guided process approach** develops learners' confidence in planning, drafting, and editing their written work.

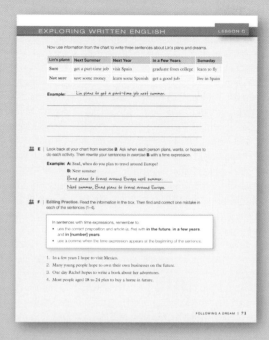

EXPLORING WRITTEN ENGLISH    LESSON C

Now use information from the chart to write three sentences about Lin's plans and dreams.

| Lin's plans | Next Summer | Next Year | In a Few Years | Someday |
|---|---|---|---|---|
| Sure | get a part-time job | visit Spain | graduate from college | learn to fly |
| Not sure | save some money | learn some Spanish | get a good job | live in Spain |

**Example:** Lin plans to get a part-time job next summer.

**E** | Look back at your chart from exercise B. Ask when each person plans, wants, or hopes to do each activity. Then rewrite your sentences in exercise B with a time expression.

**Example: A:** Brad, when do you plan to travel around Europe?
**B:** Next summer
Brad plans to travel around Europe next summer.
Next summer, Brad plans to travel around Europe.

**F** | **Editing Practice.** Read the information in the box. Then find and correct one mistake in each of the sentences (1–4).

In sentences with time expressions, remember to:
• use the correct preposition and article (i.e., the) with **in the future, in a few years,** and **in [number] years**
• use a comma when the time expression appears at the beginning of the sentence.

1. In a few years I hope to visit Mexico.
2. Many young people hope to own their own businesses in the future.
3. One day Rachel hopes to write a book about her adventures.
4. Most people aged 18 to 24 plan to buy a home in future.

FOLLOWING A DREAM | 71

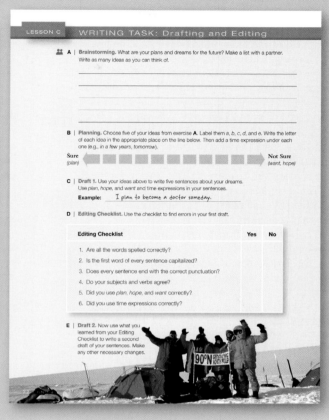

LESSON C    WRITING TASK: Drafting and Editing

**A** | **Brainstorming.** What are your plans and dreams for the future? Make a list with a partner. Write as many ideas as you can think of.

**B** | **Planning.** Choose five of your ideas from exercise **A**. Label them a, b, c, d, and e. Write the letter of each idea in the appropriate place on the line below. Then add a time expression under each one (e.g., in a few years, tomorrow).

Sure (plan) — — — — — — — Not Sure (want, hope)

**C** | **Draft 1.** Use your ideas above to write five sentences about your dreams. Use plan, hope, and want and time expressions in your sentences.
**Example:** I plan to become a doctor someday.

**D** | **Editing Checklist.** Use the checklist to find errors in your first draft.

| Editing Checklist | Yes | No |
|---|---|---|
| 1. Are all the words spelled correctly? | | |
| 2. Is the first word of every sentence capitalized? | | |
| 3. Does every sentence end with the correct punctuation? | | |
| 4. Do your subjects and verbs agree? | | |
| 5. Did you use plan, hope, and want correctly? | | |
| 6. Did you use time expressions correctly? | | |

**E** | **Draft 2.** Now use what you learned from your Editing Checklist to write a second draft of your sentences. Make any other necessary changes.

## Assessment CD-ROM with Exam*View*®

containing a bank of ready-made questions for quick and effective assessment.

## Online Workbook, powered by MyELT,

with both teacher-led and self-study options. This contains the ten National Geographic video clips, supported by interactive, automatically graded activities that practice the skills learned in the Student Books.

## Classroom Presentation Tool CD-ROM featuring audio and video

clips, and interactive activities from the Student Book. These can be used with an interactive whiteboard or computer projector.

PATHWAYS FOUNDATIONS    Unit 4: Vocabulary Practice A

Drag the correct word into each sentence. Click the words to change your answer. Scroll down. Complete all items. Then click Submit to check your answers.

plan | practice | interested in | agree | determined | happens | company

1. My father works for a _____ that produces airplanes.
2. When an important event _____, I learn about it on the Internet.
3. Mountaineers need to be very _____ to reach their goal.
4. Musicians need to _____ for many years to become successful.
5. Most scientists _____ that the global climate is changing.
6. As a child, I was _____ crocodiles and other dangerous animals.
7. My city has a new _____ to start a bike-share program.

Show Answers    Submit

## PHOTO, ILLUSTRATION and MAP CREDITS

**Front Cover:** Stephen Alvarez/NGS, **IFC:** Courtesy of Emily Ainsworth on behalf of NG, Rebecca Hale/NGC, Frederick M. Brown/Getty Images, Courtesy of Albert Lin on behalf of NG, Felix Hörhager/dpa/Corbis, Courtesy of Lana Eklund, Art & Soul Photography Inc., Courtesy of Mariana Fuentes on behalf of NG, Joel Sartore/NGC, **i:** Brian J. Skerry/NGC, **iii:** Randy Olson/NGC, Xavier Coll Sola/NGC, Paul Chesley/NGC, Courtesy of Emily Ainsworth on behalf of NG, Courtesy of Albert Lin on behalf of NGC, Joel Sartore/NGC, muslimhertiageimages.com, Dana Berry/NGC, **iv:** Courtesy of Emily Ainsworth on behalf of NG, Robert Sullivan/AFP/Getty Images, Richard Nowitz/NGC, Joel Sartore/NGC, **iv-v:** NASA Goddard Space Flight Center Image by Reto Stöckli (land surface, shallow water, clouds), **v:** Bobby Model/NGC, muslimhertiageimages.com, Courtesy of Albert Lin on behalf of NGC, Courtesy of Mariana Fuentes on behalf of NG, **vi:** Randy Olson/NGC, Gordon Wiltsie/NGC, Gordon Wiltsie/NGC, Paul Chesley/NGC, Borge Ousland/NGC, **viii:** Courtesy of Albert Lin on behalf of NGC, Linda Drake/My Shot/NGC, muslimhertiageimages.com, Darlyne A. Murawski/NGC, **1:** Randy Olson/NGC, **2:** Nigel Holmes/NGC, **3:** Amy Riley/iStockphoto.com, **5:** Randy Olson/NGC, **6:** Prof. Stan Z. Li and his research team of the Center for Biometrics and Security Research, **9:** Randy Olson/NGC, **19:** Gordon Wiltsie/NGC, **20-21:** Jimmy Chin and Lynsey Dyer/NGC, **24:** Xavier Coll Sola/NGC, **25:** Tino Soriano/NGC, **27:** Brady Barr/NGC, **28:** Michael Nichols/NGC, **30:** Bobby Model/NGC, **31:** Red Bull Stratos/EPA/Newscom, **31:** Brian J. Skerry/NGC, **37:** Paul Chesley/NGC, **39:** Bruce Dale/NGC, **42:** Jason Edwards/NGC, **43:** Tyrone Turner/NG, **45:** California State Revenue & Management Agency/NGC, **48-49:** Alvaro Valino/NGC, **49:** Richard Nowitz/NGC, **55:** Borge Ousland/NGC, **56-57:** Aaron Lim Boon Teck/NGC, **59:** Robert Sullivan/AFP/Getty Images, **62:** Michael Nichols/NGC, **63:** AP Photo/Richard A. Carioti, **64:** Paul Kane/Getty Images, **66-68:** Courtesy of Emily Ainsworth on behalf of NG, **72:** Borge Ousland/NGC, **73:** Alex Matthews/Qualcomm Institute/UC San Diego, **74-75:** NG Maps, **77:** Courtesy of Albert Lin on behalf of NGC, **78:** William H. Bond/NGC, **78:** James L. Stanfield/NGC **80:** James L. Stanfield/NGC, **81:** Courtesy of Albert Lin on behalf of NGC, **84:** AP Photo/Farmers Museum, HO, **85:** Jason Neely/My Shot/NGC, **85:** Melissa Brandts/My Shot/NGC, **91:** Michael Nichols/NGC, **92:** Linda Drake/My Shot/NGC, **92:** Sarah Connor/My Shot/NGC, **92:** Joel Sartore/NGC, **92-93:** Joel Sartore/NGC, **94:** Thinkstock/Thinkstock, **95:** George Grall/NGC, **96:** Courtesy of Mariana Fuentes on behalf of NG, **96:** Steve Winter/NGC, **98-100, 102-103:** (All) Joel Sartore/NGC, **103:** Ivy Close Images/Alamy, **104-105:** Joel Sartore/NGC, **106:** Courtesy of Mariana Fuentes on behalf of NG, **106:** Joel Sartore/NGC, **111:** muslimhertiageimages.com, **112-113:** Robert Sisson/NGC, **113:** Hulton Archive/Getty Images, **114:** JT Vintage/Glasshouse Images/Alamy, **115-116, 118-119:** (All) muslimhertiageimages.com, **120:** Paul Chesley/NG, **122:** SSPL/Getty Images, **123:** Mark Dunn/Alamy, **124:** SSPL/Getty Images, **126:** phant/iStockphoto.com, **126:** Comstock/Comstock Images/Getty Images, **126:** Diana Taliun/Shutterstock.com, **129:** Darlyne A. Murawski/NGC, **130-131:** NG Maps/NG, **131:** NASA/CXC/MIT/F.K.BAGANOFF/NGC, **131:** Ammit Jack/Shutterstock.com, **131:** ESO/NGC, **133:** Dana Berry/NGC **134:** Stephan Martiniere/NGC, **137:** Wes C. Skiles/NGC, **140-141:** Brian J. Skerry/NGC, **141:** Joe Stancampiano/NGC, **141:** Darlyne A. Muraeski/NGC, **141:** Jason Edwards/NGC, **141:** Emory Kristof/NGC, **141:** Brian J. Skerry/NGC, **141:** George Grall/NGC, **141:** Brian J. Skerry/NGC, **141:** Paul Zahl/NGC, **151:** Joel Sartore/NGC, **159:** Joel Sartore/NGC

## TEXT CREDITS/SOURCES

**5-6:** Adapted from "The Face of Seven Billion": http://ngm.nationalgeographic.com/2011/03/age-of-man/face-interactive; **12-13:** Source: State of the Media: The Social Media Report 2012: http://www.nielsen.com; **24-25:** Adapted from "Teenage Brains": NGM Oct 2011. Additional sources of information: "Are You a Risk Taker?": http://ngm.nationalgeographic.com/2011/10/teenage-brains/, and "Fear Factor: Success and Risk in Extreme Sports": http://news.nationalgeographic.com/; **30-31:** Adapted from "Kira Salak": http://www.nationalgeographic.com/explorers/bios/kira-salak/, "Space Dive Success": http://news.nationalgeographic.com/news/2012/10/121014-felix-baumgartner-skydive-sound-barrier-kittinger-roswell-science-2/, and "Brian Skerry": http://photography.nationalgeographic.com/photography/photographers/photographer-brian-skerry/; **42-43:** Adapted from "NG Weekend: Interview with Taras Grescoe": http://radio.nationalgeographic.com/radio/ng-weekend-archives/1227/; **48-49:** Adapted from "Bike-Share Schemes Shift Into High Gear": http://news.nationalgeographic.com/news/energy/2011/06/110607-global-bike-share/, and "City Solution: Bike Sharing": NGM June 2012; **59-60:** Adapted from "Barrington Irving": http://www.nationalgeographic.com/explorers/bios/barrington-irving; **66-67:** Adapted from "Emily Ainsworth": http://www.nationalgeographic.com/explorers/bios/emily-ainsworth/, "Explorer of the Week": http://newswatch.nationalgeographic.com/2012/08/29/explorer-of-the-week-emily-ainsworth/, and "Behind the Mexican Circus": http://newswatch.nationalgeographic.com/2012/05/23/behind-the-mexican-circus-with-young-explorer-emily-ainsworth/; **77-78:** Adapted from "Albert Lin": http://www.nationalgeographic.com/explorers/bios/albert-lin/, "The Valley of the Khans Project": http://www.nationalgeographic.com/explorers/projects/valley-khans-project/, and "Conjuring Genghis Khan": http://adventure.nationalgeographic.com/2009/12/best-of-adventure/albert-lin/1; **84-85:** Adapted from "Skeleton of Giant is Internet Hoax": http://news.nationalgeographic.com/news/bigphotos/21432885.html, and "Cheeky Squirrel Photo Crasher": http://intelligenttravel.nationalgeographic.com/2009/08/12/ground_squirrel_photo_crasher/; **94-96:** Adapted from "Mariana Fuentes": http://www.nationalgeographic.com/explorers/bios/mariana-fuentes/; **102-105:** Adapted from "Martha's Legacy": http://ngm.nationalgeographic.com/visions/field-test/sartore-biodiversity/dispatch-7; **115-116:** Source of information: "1001 Inventions: The Enduring Legacy of Muslim Civilization," Published by National Geographic Books, 2012; **122-123:** Adapted from "Ada Lovelace Day Celebrates Women in Science": http://newswatch.nationalgeographic.com/2012/10/16/ada-lovelace-day/; **133-134:** Adapted from "New Earths": NGM Dec 2009, and "Crazy Far": NGM Jan 2013; **140-141:** Adapted from "Sea Mounts": NGM Sep 2012.

IFC = Inside Front Cover
NGS = National Geographic Stock
NGC = National Geographic Creative
NG = National Geographic
NGM = National Geographic Magazine

# Our World

ACADEMIC PATHWAYS

## Think and Discuss

1. How many people do you think are in the world today?
2. Which countries have the most people?

▲ A crowd of people at
a festival in Puri, India

1

More than 7 billion (7,000,000,000) people are alive on Earth today.

# How Big Is Seven Billion?

7,000,000,000

*Only 132 laps to go*

= number of **steps** to walk around the Earth 133 times

Pluto

Sun

Earth

## Exploring the Theme

**A.** Look at the information on these pages and answer the questions.

    1. How many people are alive today?

    2. Which information is the most surprising?

**B.** Answer the questions about yourself.

    1. How many steps do you think you walk each day?

    2. How many text messages do you think you send each day?

    3. How many days would it take you to walk 7 billion steps?
       How many days would it take you to send 7 billion text messages?

= number of **text messages** sent in the U.S. every 30 hours

= the **age in seconds** of the world's longest-living animal, the quahog clam (about 220 years)

= number of **kilometers** from the sun to Pluto

**Word Usage**

You usually do not use **male** or **female** as nouns when you refer to people. Use *man* or *woman*. Use *male* and *female* as adjectives when you talk or write about factual information. For example: *Female chickens are called hens.*

**A** | **Building Vocabulary.** Match the sentence parts (1–5 and a–e) to make definitions. Use a dictionary to help you.

1. _____ A **human** is
2. _____ A **city** is
3. _____ Boys and men are
4. _____ Girls and women are
5. _____ A **job** is

a. a person (not an animal or a machine).
b. **male**.
c. the work that someone does to get money.
d. a large town such as New York, Tokyo, or Paris.
e. **female**.

**B** | **Building Vocabulary.** Read the definitions. Use the words in blue **bold** to complete the sentences (1–5).

**Word Partners**

Use **common** with nouns or the preposition *in*: (n.) common **language**, common **interest**, common **culture**, common **beliefs**, (*prep.*) (to have something) **in** common.

A **nation** is a country such as the United States or China.
If something is **common**, it happens often, or you find it in large numbers.
If things are put **together**, they touch each other or make a single object or group.
A **few** means some, but not many.
If two people or things are **different**, they are not like each other.

1. In 2010, the most _____ male name in Japan was Ren.

2. Thai food is very _____ from British food. Thai food is hot and spicy, but British food is not.

3. East Germany and West Germany were two countries, but in 1990 they came _____ to make one country.

4. Every _____ has its own flag. The Italian flag has green, white, and red stripes on it.

5. The country of Tuvalu is very small. It is only a _____ miles wide.

**C** | **Using Vocabulary.** Answer the questions (1–4). Share your ideas with a partner.

1. What is the name of your favorite **city**?
2. What **job** do you want to have in five years?
3. What are some **common** jobs among people that you know?
4. Name a **few** of your favorite foods.

**D** | **Predicting.** Read the title and look at the photos on pages 5 and 6. What do you think the reading is mainly about? Circle your answer.

1. a typical person today     2. a typical day on Earth     3. life in a typical city

# The Human Planet

track 1-01

**A**    **The world's population** grows faster every decade. In the year 1800, there were 1 billion people in the world. There are now over 7 billion people on the planet. By 2045, there may be 9 billion. Every second, five people are born and two people die.

**B**    What are some characteristics[1] of a typical **human** today? Earth is now an urban planet: More people—51 percent of the population—live in a **city** than in the countryside. More humans are **male** than **female**, but only by a small majority: There are 1.01 men in the world for every woman. The world's population is mostly young: The 28-year-old age group is the largest.

**C**    About 82 percent of the world's population can read and write. Forty percent of the population works in service **jobs,** for example, restaurant and hotel workers. More people work on farms (30 percent) than in industry (22 percent).

[1] **Characteristics** are qualities or features that are typical of someone or something.

▲ Rows of houses in Huaxi, China

D

China, with over 1.3 billion people, is the **nation** with the largest population. The largest ethnic group[2] is Han Chinese. The most **common** language in the world today is Mandarin. About 13 percent of the world's population speaks Mandarin as a first language.

E

Some researchers at the Chinese Academy of Sciences in Beijing created a picture of the typical man and woman. They used thousands of photos of 28-year-old Han Chinese men and women. They put them **together** to make photos of the typical male and female on Earth today.

F

The world's population is still growing and changing. In a **few** years, the typical person may be very **different**: In 2030, he (or she) will probably be from India.

[2] An **ethnic group** is a group of people from one race or culture.

The "typical" human is a 28-year-old Han Chinese male. He lives in a city, can read and write, speaks Mandarin, and has a service job.

▲ Researchers in Beijing created these images of the typical woman and man on the planet today.

**A** | **Understanding the Gist.** Look back at your answer for exercise **D** on page 4.
Was your prediction correct?

**B** | **Identifying Key Details.** Complete each sentence (1–7) with the correct number from the reading.

1.  There were about 1 billion people on the planet in the year _____.

2.  There will probably be 9 billion people in the year _____.

3.  About _____ percent of people live in a city.

4.  For every woman on Earth, there are _____ men.

5.  The most common age of people living today is _____.

6.  About _____ percent of people have service jobs.

7.  The typical person may be from India by the year _____.

**C** | **Critical Thinking: Guessing Meaning from Context.** Find and underline the following words in the reading on pages 5–6. Use the context—the words around the word—to help you understand its meaning.

> **population** (paragraph A)   **urban** (paragraph B)   **majority** (paragraph B)
> **industry** (paragraph C)   **probably** (paragraph F)

Complete each definition with the correct word from the box. Check your answers in a dictionary.

1.  An _____ is usually a type of business that makes things, for example, cars or computers.

2.  The _____ of a country or an area is all the people who live in it.

3.  If something is _____ true, you think it is true, but you are not sure.

4.  _____ means being part of a city or a town.

5.  The _____ of people or things in a group is more than half of them.

**D** | **Critical Thinking: Reflecting.** Complete the chart with information about the typical person and about yourself. When the two answers are the same, put a check (✓) in the third column. Then compare your answers with a partner.

| | Typical person | You | Same Answer? |
|---|---|---|---|
| Urban or countryside? | urban | | |
| Job? | | (now or in the future) | |
| First language? | | | |
| Age? | | | |
| Male or female? | | | |
| Nation or ethnic group? | | | |

**CT Focus**

When you **reflect** on ideas and information you connect them with your own experience. Ask yourself these questions as you read: *What do I think about this? How does this relate to my life?*

**Reading Skill:** *Identifying Purpose*

As you read a passage, think about why the writer wrote it.

- to entertain?
- to share an opinion?
- to sell something?
- to inform and give facts?
- for a different purpose?

Thinking about the writer's purpose may help you better understand what he or she is saying.
If the writer is sharing an opinion, ask yourself this question: Do I agree with the writer?
If the writer wants to sell something, ask yourself this question: Do I believe this information?

**A | Identifying Purpose.** Read the paragraphs below and match each paragraph to its purpose.

1. to inform     2. to share an opinion     3. to sell something

track **1-02**

_____ Medical care is very advanced now, but many people in poorer countries do not have good health care. I think rich countries should give money to poorer countries to improve their health care. With better health care, people all over the world could live longer, healthier, and happier lives.

_____ Birthrates and life spans are very different now than they were in the past. People had more children in the past. One reason for this is that many children died in childbirth or when they were very young. Now, better medical care means more babies and children survive, so people have fewer babies. Better health care and nutrition also help us all live longer. In 1960, the average person lived 52 years. Now, the average person lives 69 years.

_____ Most of us have good medical care and nutritious food these days, but we still have to take care of our own health. Eating good food and exercising is not enough. We don't get enough vitamins and minerals from our food. Big Life vitamins and minerals can help. Thousands of people have tried Big Life vitamins, and they feel better, look better, and live longer.

**B | Identifying Purpose.** Think about the reading on pages 5–6. What is the writer's purpose?

a. to inform     b. to entertain     c. to share an opinion     d. to sell something

# 7 Billion

## Before Viewing

**A | Using a Dictionary.** Here are some words you will hear in the video. Complete each definition with the correct word. Use your dictionary to help you.

| adequate | average | balance | consume | energy | sanitation |
|---|---|---|---|---|---|

1. If something is _____, it is usual, typical, or normal.
2. If something is _____, there is enough of it or it is good enough.
3. When you _____ something, you use it, eat it, or drink it.
4. _____ is a situation when two or more things have the same weight or importance.
5. _____ is the process of keeping things clean and healthy, for example, water and toilets.
6. _____ is the strength or power that makes things work.

**B | Thinking Ahead.** Look back at the information on pages 2–3. Then complete the sentence with your own guess.

It takes about _____ years to count to 7 billion.

## While Viewing

Read the sentences (1–5). What information is missing? Listen for the answers as you view the video.

1. A megacity is a city with _____ or more people in it.
2. In 1975, there were _____ of these cities, and now there are _____.
3. All 7 billion people could fit in the city of _____.
4. Five percent of the population uses 23 percent of the world's _____.
5. Thirteen percent of people don't have clean _____.

## After Viewing

**A |** Discuss the answers to the statements (1-5) above with a partner.

**B | Critical Thinking: Synthesizing.** What information in the video matches information in the reading on pages 5–6? Check (✔) the information that is in the reading and the video.

☐ 1. There were 1 billion people in the world in 1800.
☐ 2. Every second, five people are born and two people die.
☐ 3. Eighty-two percent of people can read and write.
☐ 4. Mandarin is the most common language in the world.
☐ 5. Most people today live in cities.

**A** | **Building Vocabulary.** Read the definitions below. Then complete each sentence (1-5) with the correct word or phrase.

If something is **increasing**, it is getting bigger.

A million, or one **million**, is the number 1,000,000.

If something happens **instantly**, it happens very quickly or immediately.

**Habits** are things we do often or regularly.

If you **connect with** people, you communicate with them.

1. The sun is about 150 _____ kilometers from Earth.

2. Many people _____ friends online. They often send messages to each other on social networks such as Facebook.

3. Researchers studied the travel _____ of people in big cities. Many people in big cities usually take public transportation to get to work.

4. The number of people working in health care is _____ in my city. Ten years ago, there were 500 nurses in my city. Now, there are 2,000.

5. I don't wait for the news on television or go out to buy a newspaper. I like to get information _____, so I read the news online.

**B** | **Building Vocabulary.** Read the sentences below. Write each word in **bold** next to its definition (1–5).

In the 1940s, computers were the size of large rooms. **However**, many computers are now small enough to hold in your hand.

Facebook and Twitter are two very **popular** social networking sites. Many people go online to tell friends about **social** events such as parties or shows.

Some people are **constantly** on their cell phones. They talk and text all day long.

If someone finds out your password for an Internet site, make sure you **change** it to something else.

1. _____: happening all the time

2. _____: to make something different

3. _____: liked by a lot of people

4. _____: but; yet; on the other hand

5. _____: relating to society; involving other people

**C | Using Vocabulary.** Answer the questions (1–4) in complete sentences. Then share your answers with a partner.

1. Do you think you have good study **habits**? Give an example.

   _____

   _____

2. How do you usually **connect with** your friends?

   _____

   _____

3. What is the most **popular** television show in your country?

   _____

   _____

4. Do you ever **change** your Internet passwords? Why, or why not?

   _____

   _____

**Word Partners**

Use **habits** with a noun: **communication** habits, **sleep** habits, **travel** habits, **work** habits.

**D | Expanding Vocabulary.** Complete the chart with the missing words. Then use a dictionary to check your answers.

| Adjectives | Adverbs | Adjectives | Adverbs |
|---|---|---|---|
| | constantly | quick | |
| easy | | quiet | |
| | instantly | social | |

**Word Link**

You can add the suffix **-ly** to some adjectives to make adverbs, e.g., constant**ly**, loud**ly**, sad**ly**, slow**ly**, sudden**ly**.

Now write four sentences using words from the chart.

1. _____

2. _____

3. _____

4. _____

**E | Predicting.** Look at the title, subheads, and graphics in the reading on pages 12–13. What do you think the writer's purpose is?

a. to inform       b. to entertain       c. to share an opinion

# HOW DO WE COMMUNICATE?

**How do you connect with social networking sites? (%)**

Chart data:

COMPUTER: 93, 96, 91, 96, 94
CELL PHONE: 59, 33, 48, 33, 46
TABLET: 28, 8, 10, 6, 16
GAME CONSOLE: 5, 3, 2, 3, 4
HANDHELD MUSIC PLAYER: 5, 2, 2, 2, 7

Legend: ASIA-PACIFIC | EUROPE | M. EAST/AFRICA | LATIN AMERICA | NORTH AMERICA

track 1-03

**A**  The world's population is **increasing** every year, but in some ways the world is getting smaller, not larger. Now, **millions** of people around the world can communicate easily and quickly in many different ways. For example, computers, smartphones, and tablets can bring people together **instantly**.

**B**  How are these new types of communication changing our lives? In 2012, the Nielsen Research Group studied the communication **habits** of 28,000 people worldwide. Above are some of their findings.

## Do you use social networking sites while watching TV?

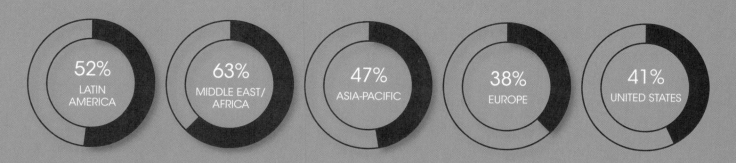

| 52% LATIN AMERICA | 63% MIDDLE EAST/ AFRICA | 47% ASIA-PACIFIC | 38% EUROPE | 41% UNITED STATES |

## How much time do you spend social networking?
### IN HOURS AND MINUTES (HH:MM) PER MONTH (United States)

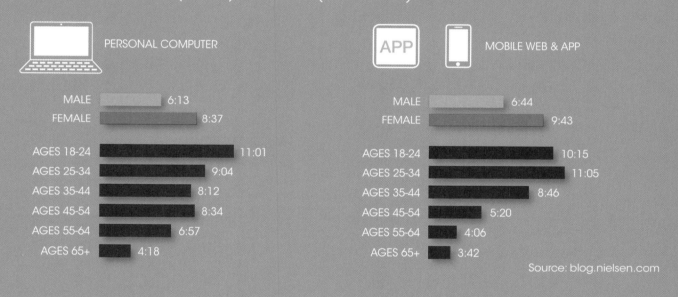

**PERSONAL COMPUTER**

| | |
|---|---|
| MALE | 6:13 |
| FEMALE | 8:37 |
| AGES 18-24 | 11:01 |
| AGES 25-34 | 9:04 |
| AGES 35-44 | 8:12 |
| AGES 45-54 | 8:34 |
| AGES 55-64 | 6:57 |
| AGES 65+ | 4:18 |

**MOBILE WEB & APP**

| | |
|---|---|
| MALE | 6:44 |
| FEMALE | 9:43 |
| AGES 18-24 | 10:15 |
| AGES 25-34 | 11:05 |
| AGES 35-44 | 8:46 |
| AGES 45-54 | 5:20 |
| AGES 55-64 | 4:06 |
| AGES 65+ | 3:42 |

Source: blog.nielsen.com

C  The majority of people **connect with** other people online using a computer. **However**, other types of communication are becoming **popular**. In Asia-Pacific, for example, almost 60 percent of people use a cell phone to connect with **social** media sites. About 28 percent connect from a tablet. In the United States, the typical mobile user of social media is female, between the ages of 25 and 34.

D  Many people communicate online almost **constantly** throughout the day. People often use social networking sites while they do something else. In Latin America, more than 50 percent of people visit social networking sites while they watch TV.

E  Today, more people can communicate with each other than ever before. This is very different from just 50 years ago. How will communication **change** our lives in the next 50 years?

**A** | **Understanding Purpose.** Look back at your answer for exercise **E** on page 11. Was your prediction correct?

**B** | **Identifying the Main Ideas.** Match each of these main ideas with a paragraph (A–E) from the reading on pages 12–13.

_____ 1. Communication habits have changed a lot in 50 years, and may be very different in the future.

_____ 2. Most people go online using a computer, but other ways are becoming popular.

_____ 3. There are more people in the world now, but in some ways the world is getting smaller.

**C** | **Identifying Key Details.** Complete each sentence (1–4) with information from pages 12–13.

1. Ninety-six percent of people in _____ and _____ connect with social networking sites using a computer.

2. _____ of people in the Middle East and Africa use social networking sites while watching TV.

3. A typical male computer user spends _____ hours and _____ minutes a month on social networking sites.

4. People aged _____ spend the most time social networking from mobile devices.

**D** | **Critical Thinking: Guessing Meaning from Context.** Find and underline the following words in the reading passage on pages 12–13. Complete each definition with the correct word. Check your answers in a dictionary.

> **research** (paragraph B)     **findings** (paragraph B)     **mobile** (paragraph C)

1. If you are _____, you can move or travel easily from place to place.

2. If you do _____, you study something to learn facts about it.

3. _____ are the facts and information you learn from doing research.

**E** | **Critical Thinking: Synthesizing and Reflecting.** Think about your answers for exercise **D** on page 7 and the information in the reading on pages 12-13. What do you have in common with the typical person? Discuss your answer in a small group.

**GOAL:** In this lesson, you are going to draft and edit sentences on the following topic:
***Describe yourself and your communication habits.***

**A** | Read the information below.

## Language for Writing: What Is a Sentence?

A **sentence** is a group of words that expresses an idea. Sentences begin with capital letters and end with punctuation marks such as periods (.), question marks (?), and exclamation points (!).

A sentence must have at least one subject and one verb:

The **subject** is the person or thing that does the action.

The **verb** is usually the action word.

For example, look at these sentences:

*Many people communicate online almost constantly throughout the day.*

*The largest ethnic group is Han Chinese.*

*Every second, five people are born and two people die.*

Most sentences also include words such as adjectives (*largest*), adverbs (*constantly*), prepositions (*throughout*), and connecting words (*and*).

If a sentence does not have a subject and a verb, it is a fragment.
Here are two examples. What is missing in each one?

*Created a picture of the typical man and woman.*

*The 28-year-old age group the largest.*

Now underline the subject and circle the verb in each sentence (1–5).
(Two sentences have more than one subject and verb.)

1. I use my phone every day.

2. We don't call each other very often.

3. Every day, my friends send me emails or texts.

4. He always goes online when he's watching TV.

5. I connect on my phone when I don't have my laptop.

**B** | Read the items below (1–7). Check (✓) each complete sentence. If it is a fragment, what is missing? Write **S** for *subject* or **V** for *verb*.

☐  1.  In 2030, the typical person probably from India. _____

☐  2.  The population gets bigger every year. _____

☐  3.  Cell phones are also known as mobile phones. _____

☐  4.  Researchers thousands of photos of 28-year-old people. _____

☐  5.  Lives in a big city, not a small country town. _____

☐  6.  My school's library has 50 computers for students. _____

☐  7.  I never the computers in the library. _____

**C** | Unscramble the words to make sentences. Then underline the subjects and circle the verbs.

1.  cell phones / people / A lot of / have / .

_____

2.  have / landlines / people / Not a lot of / .

_____

3.  all over / Internet / the world / use the / People from / .

_____

4.  are / heavy / not very / Tablets / .

_____

**D** | Read the information below. Then complete each sentence (1–6 on page 17) with the correct form of *be*. Do not use contractions.

**Language for Writing:** Simple Present Tense of *be*

We use the simple present for habits, daily routines, facts, or things that are generally true. We use the verb *be* to describe people, things, and situations.

The simple present tense of *be* has three forms: *am*, *is*, and *are*. Using the correct verb form with a subject is called "subject-verb agreement."

I ⟶ **am / 'm**
he / she / it ⟶ **is / 's**
you / we / they ⟶ **are / 're**

We usually use nouns, adjectives, or prepositional phrases after *be*.

*I am a* **student**.    *I like Pinterest. It's* **fun**.    *The tablets are* **on the desk**.

1. My brothers _____ in Seoul.

2. My sister _____ a doctor.

3. I _____ in law school.

4. My favorite social networking site _____ Tagged.

5. I think it _____ a great way to meet people.

6. Facebook and Twitter _____ fun, too.

E | Read the information below.

**Language for Writing:** Simple Present Tense of Other Verbs

For verbs other than *be*, use the base form with *I, you, we,* and *they*. For most verbs, use the base form + -s with *he, she,* and *it*.

| | | |
|---|---|---|
| I **like** Pinterest. | She **likes** Pinterest. | We **like** Pinterest. |
| I **use** Twitter. | Mark (or He) **uses** Twitter. | Kim and Leo (or They) **use** Twitter. |

If a verb ends in -*y,* drop the -*y* and add -*ies*.

| | | |
|---|---|---|
| I **study** at night. | Kay **studies** in the morning. | They **study** after lunch. |

Some verbs do not follow the usual rule. You do not use the base form + -s with *he, she,* and *it*. Instead, these verbs have irregular forms.

She **does** her homework on a tablet.
Alex **goes** to school at 9:00 A.M.
Tomas **has** a laptop, a tablet, and a smartphone.

For further explanation and more examples, see page 155.

Now complete each pair of sentences (1–5) with a verb from the box. Use the simple present.

| like | live | speak | study | use |
|---|---|---|---|---|

1. I _____ science for about two hours every day.

   My sister _____ for about three hours a day.

2. I _____ Twitter better than Facebook.

   Joe _____ Facebook better than Twitter.

3. Pam and Luke _____ in the country.

   Alex _____ in the city.

4. Tina _____ three languages: Spanish, French, and English.

   I _____ two languages: English and Mandarin.

5. Matt and Kim _____ the computers in the library.

   Sometimes James _____ the computers in the coffee shop.

**A** | **Brainstorming.** Write answers to the questions (1–6). Write notes (not complete sentences). Share your answers with a partner.

**About yourself:**

1. Where do you live?

   _____

2. What languages do you speak?

   _____

3. Do you have a job? If yes, what is it? If not, what do you want to do?

   _____

**About your communication habits:**

4. How do you connect with friends online?

   _____

5. How long do you spend on social media in a typical day?

   _____

6. What websites do you like?

   _____

**B** | **Planning.** Look at your ideas in exercise **A**. Add some other facts about yourself and your communication habits.

**C** | **Draft 1.** Use the information above to write four sentences about yourself and your communication habits. Use the simple present tense of *be* and other verbs in your sentences.

   **Example:** I live in Tokyo, Japan.

**D** | **Editing Checklist.** Use the checklist to find errors in your first draft.

| Editing Checklist | Yes | No |
|---|---|---|
| 1.  Are all the words spelled correctly? |  |  |
| 2.  Is the first word of every sentence capitalized? |  |  |
| 3.  Does every sentence end with the correct punctuation? |  |  |
| 4.  Does each sentence have a subject and a verb? |  |  |
| 5.  Did you use the simple present tense correctly? |  |  |
| 6.  Do your subjects and verbs agree? |  |  |

**E** | **Draft 2.** Now use what you learned from your Editing Checklist to write a second draft of your sentences. Make any necessary changes.

# Risk Takers

ACADEMIC PATHWAYS
Lesson A: Previewing
            Analyzing sources
Lesson B: Reading biographical profiles
Lesson C: Writing sentences about risk taking

▲ Risk-taking
mountaineers
on Baffin Island,
Canada, sleep
in tents hanging
from ropes.

## Think and Discuss

1. "Taking a risk" means doing
   something dangerous or uncertain.
   What risks do you sometimes take?

2. What kinds of people take a lot of
   risks in their lives?

## Exploring the Theme

**A.** Look at the photo and answer the questions.

1. What are the people doing?

2. What kind of people do you think they are? Describe them.

**B.** Read the information below and answer the questions.

1. What are two characteristics of risk takers?

2. Who is more likely to take risks—males or females? Younger people or older people?

## What Is a Risk Taker?

Risk takers know something bad can happen, but they don't worry about it. A skydiver—a person who jumps from an airplane as a sport— is an example of a risk taker. Of course, it can be dangerous to jump from an airplane. But a risk taker *enjoys* this type of danger.

Psychologists—scientists who study the human mind—say that most risk takers become bored easily. So they enjoy the excitement of a risk. Who takes risks? Psychologists say males usually take more risks than females. The greatest risk takers are teenage males.

◄ BASE jumpers take risks when they jump from buildings, bridges, or mountains. BASE jumpers use a parachute to stop their fall. These BASE jumpers are jumping from Half Dome in Yosemite National Park, USA.

**A** | **Building Vocabulary.** Match the sentence parts (1–5 and a–e) to make definitions. Use a dictionary to check your answers.

| | |
|---|---|
| 1. _____ If something is **dangerous,** | a. you are sure about it. |
| | b. they make it easier for you to do something. |
| 2. _____ A **career** | c. it may harm you. |
| 3. _____ If you are **confident** about something, | d. is what is happening in a particular place at a particular time. |
| 4. _____ If things **help,** | e. is a job, for example, working as a doctor. |
| 5. _____ A **situation** | |

**Word Partners**

Use **goal** with verbs and adjectives: (*v.*) **have** a goal, **share** a goal; (*adj.*) **personal** goal, **main** goal.

**B** | **Building Vocabulary.** Complete the sentences (1–5) with the words in the box.

| activity | alone | business | goal | succeed |
|---|---|---|---|---|

1. To _____ in school, you need to study hard.

2. Many people don't want to work for other people. They want to have their own _____ so they can be the boss.

3. Having a common _____ helps people to work together.

4. Many people don't like to travel _____. They like to travel with other people.

5. An _____ such as walking or swimming is a good way to exercise.

**C** | **Using Vocabulary.** Answer the questions (1–3). Share your ideas with a partner.

1. Do you have a **goal** for learning English? What is it?

2. What **activities** do you enjoy the most?

3. Do you like to travel **alone** or with other people?

**D** | **Brainstorming.** With a partner, list some jobs, sports, or other activities that are dangerous.

1. _____     3. _____     5. _____

2. _skydiving_     4. _____     6. _____

**Reading Skill:** *Previewing, Part 1*

When you **preview** a reading passage, you look at it quickly before you start to read it. Previewing helps you to predict—or guess—what the reading is about. It helps you to understand ideas better when you read the passage more carefully later.

One way to preview is to **skim**—look quickly at—certain parts of a reading passage. Two parts of a passage you can skim are the following:

- **Subheads:** the titles of different sections of a reading
- **Captions:** the words that explain the pictures (Captions are usually below or next to the pictures.)

**A** | **Previewing.** Skim the reading passage on pages 24–25. Read the subheads. Answer these questions (1–3).

1. How many subheads are there? _____

2. Which word do you see three times in the subheads?

_____

3. a. Which subhead is a question?     1st     2nd     3rd

   b. Guess the answer to the question. Work with a partner and complete this sentence:

   *Maybe people take risks because* _____.

**B** | **Previewing.** Look at the two pictures. What are the people doing? Now read the captions. Were your guesses correct?

**C** | **Predicting.** Discuss these questions with a partner.

1. What is the passage on pages 24–25 mainly about?

2. What are two main types of risk takers you will read about?

3. What examples of risk taking do you think you will read about?

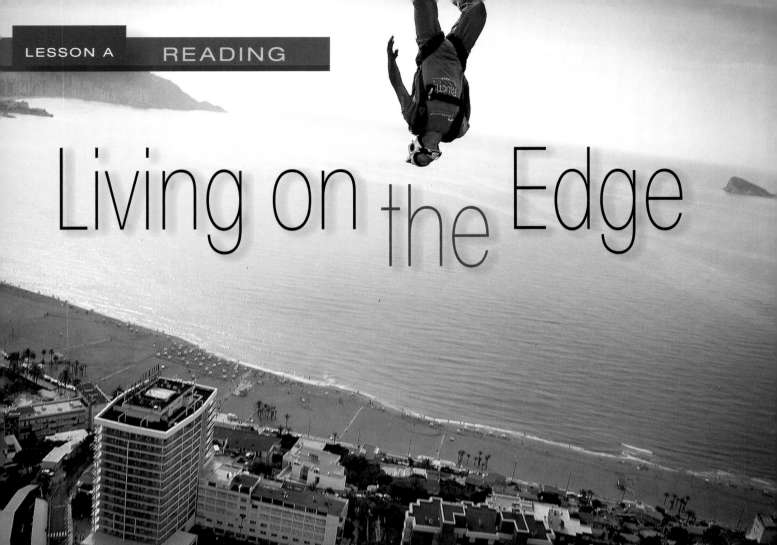

# Living on the Edge

▲ A competitor at the BASE Jump Extreme World Championship jumps from a hotel roof.

track 1-04

**A**   **Some people run** through a city with bulls chasing after them. Other people climb high mountains or travel **alone** in **dangerous** places. Why do some people enjoy risky **activities** like these?

## Why Do People Take Risks?

**B**   Risk takers have some common characteristics, experts[1] believe. For example, psychologist Marvin Zuckerman says that risk takers are always looking for change and excitement. They also feel **confident** in dangerous **situations**.

**C**   A chemical in the brain called dopamine may be related to[2] risk taking. When people do something risky, this chemical creates a pleasant feeling. Dopamine makes people feel good, so they want to do more risky activities.

---

[1] **Experts** are people who know a lot about a particular subject.
[2] If a thing is **related to** another thing, it is connected with it.

## Professional Risk Takers

▲ Every year, people in Pamplona, Spain, risk their lives by running with bulls during a festival.

D People who enjoy dangerous sports are risk takers. Extreme³ athletes see the world in a different way, says sports psychologist Shane Murphy. In a dangerous activity such as skydiving, most people probably do not feel in control.⁴ Extreme athletes are the opposite: They feel in control in dangerous situations. The danger can **help** them. For example, skier Daron Rahlves says that fear makes him try harder to **succeed**.

E Some people take risks to achieve a **goal**. Conservationist⁵ Michael Fay led a dangerous 2,000-mile expedition in central Africa. His goal was to help save the wildlife there. Fay's expedition helped to create 13 national parks.

## Everyday Risk Takers

F Most of us are not extreme athletes or explorers. However, we all like some excitement in our lives. In fact, most people are risk takers in some way. Some people take social risks, such as speaking in front of a large group of people or talking to people you don't know at a party. Some people take financial risks, such as buying a house or putting money into stocks.⁶ Other people take **career** risks, such as leaving their job and starting their own **business**. Studies show that most people take risks in some areas of life, but not in others. What kind of risk taker are you?

³ If something is **extreme**, it is very great, or more than others.
⁴ If you are **in control** of something, you have power over it.
⁵ A **conservationist** works to take care of the environment.
⁶ **Stocks** are parts of the value of a company.

**A** | **Understanding Purpose.** Look back at your answers for exercise **C** on page 23. Were your predictions correct?

**B** | **Identifying Main Ideas.** Match each main idea (1–5) to one of these paragraphs from the reading: B, C, D, E, and F.

_____ 1. Extreme athletes are different from most people.

_____ 2. Many risk takers have similar characteristics.

_____ 3. Most people take some risks in their everyday lives.

_____ 4. Some people have an important reason for taking risks.

_____ 5. Risk taking may be related to a chemical in the brain.

**C** | **Identifying Key Details.** Complete the statements (1–6) with details from the reading on pages 24–25.

1. A chemical called _____ may explain why some people take risks.

2. Extreme athletes often feel _____ in dangerous situations.

3. Michael Fay took risks to help save _____ in central Africa.

4. Speaking to people you don't know is an example of a _____ risk.

5. Buying stocks is an example of a _____ risk.

6. An example of a career risk is leaving your _____.

**D** | **Critical Thinking: Guessing Meaning from Context.** Find and underline the following words in the reading on pages 24–25. Use the context to help you understand the meaning.

> **pleasant** (paragraph C)        **expedition** (paragraph E)
> **social** (paragraph F)          **financial** (paragraph F)

Now match the words with their definitions (1–4). Check your answers in a dictionary.

1. _____: a trip that has a special goal

2. _____: relating to groups of people

3. _____: relating to money

4. _____: enjoyable

**CT Focus**

Writers often **paraphrase**— say in their own words— the ideas of experts. This gives support to the writer's ideas. For example: *[expert's name] thinks/says [that]* . . .

**E** | **Critical Thinking: Analyzing.** Find and circle the names of two experts in the reading on pages 24–25. Discuss the questions with a partner.

1. What is each person's job?

2. What main idea does each person's idea help to explain?

**F** | **Critical Thinking: Reflecting.** Think of a time when you took a risk. What type of risk was it—social, financial, career, or another type? Why did you take the risk? Discuss your ideas with a partner.

# KiLLER CROCS

## Before Viewing

**A |** **Using a Dictionary.** Here are some words you will hear in the video. Complete each definition with the correct word. Use your dictionary to help you.

| aggressive | ranger | rescue | rip | snare |

1. A _____ is a trap for catching animals.

2. A _____ takes care of a forest or a large park.

3. If you _____ off something, you tear it off.

4. If you _____ someone or something, you save it from danger.

5. An _____ person or animal behaves in a forceful or violent way.

**B |** **Brainstorming.** The video is about crocodiles that are attacking people in a village in Uganda. What do you think people in the village can do to stop crocodiles from killing people? Share your ideas with a partner.

## While Viewing

As you view the video, read each statement (1–3) and circle **T** for *true* and **F** for *false*.

1. The crocodiles are aggressive because people are killing the crocs and eating them.  **T**  **F**

2. Dr. Barr is teaching the rangers how to kill crocodiles.  **T**  **F**

3. The rangers want to protect both crocodiles and people.  **T**  **F**

## After Viewing

**A |** Discuss the statements (1–3) above with a partner. Correct the false statement(s).

**B |** **Synthesizing.** Think about the types of risk takers you read about in Lesson **A**. What kind of risk takers are Dr. Barr and the rangers?

As a wildlife expert and TV presenter, ▶ Dr. Brady Barr faces crocodiles and other dangerous animals. Here he is holding the the jaws of a wild alligator.

**A | Building Vocabulary.** Circle the correct word to complete each sentence (1–10).

1. If you **challenge / experience** something, it happens to you.

2. If something is **close / important** to you, it is near you.

3. When you **protect / challenge** yourself, you try to do something difficult.

4. If a thing is in **character / trouble**, it has problems.

5. If something is **important / enough**, it is valuable or necessary.

6. If you **protect / experience** someone or something, you keep that person or thing safe.

7. If you have **hope / enough** of something, you have as much as you need.

8. Your **character / experience** is your personality—what you are like as a person.

9. If you **challenge / hope** for something, you want it to happen.

10. **Character / Speed** is very fast movement or travel.

◄ Conservationist Michael Fay has risked his life several times on expeditions in central Africa.

**B** | **Using Vocabulary.** Answer the questions (1–3) in complete sentences. Then share your answers with a partner.

1. In what ways could you **challenge** yourself? Give an example.

   _____

2. What is an **important** thing you have learned in this class so far?

   _____

3. If a friend is having **trouble** learning a new language, how can you help him or her?

   _____

**C** | **Expanding Vocabulary.** Read the following sentence pairs (1–6). Write **N** if the **bold** word is a *noun* and **V** if the bold word is a *verb*.

1. a. Moving to a new country can be a big **challenge** for some people. _____

   b. When you learn a new language, you **challenge** yourself. _____

2. a. Michael Fay **hopes** to save wildlife in central Africa. _____

   b. "I have one **hope**," the photographer said. "I want my photographs to make people think." _____

3. a. The top **speed** for free-fall skydiving is over 800 miles per hour. _____

   b. It is very dangerous to **speed** on a busy city street. _____

4. a. Many people **experience** risk in their everyday lives. _____

   b. Some risk takers feel good when they have dangerous **experiences**. _____

5. a. A **risk** that some teenagers take is driving too fast. _____

   b. Most people drive carefully because they don't want to **risk** their lives. _____

6. a. A good **photograph** can change the way people think about something. _____

   b. Tom Sanders has a risky job. He **photographs** people jumping out of planes. _____

> **Word Usage**
>
> Using context can help you decide a word's part of speech. **Challenge** can be both a noun and a verb:
> (*n.*) **accept a** challenge, **take a** challenge;
> (*v.*) challenge **yourself**, challenge **someone** (e.g., in a game).

**D** | **Previewing and Predicting.** Answer the questions with a partner.

1. Read the subheads on pages 30-31. Which words describe a job or an activity?

   _____  _____  _____

2. Look at the pictures. What is each person doing? Read the captions. Were your guesses correct?

3. What dangers do you think each person faces in their job? Make a list.

# Adventurers

track 1-05

**Adventurers and explorers** are professional risk takers. They travel through dangerous lands, encounter[1] wild animals, and **experience** extreme situations. Here are three examples of professional risk takers—on land, in the air, and underwater.

## Solo Traveler

**Kira Salak** is a traveler and a writer. But this young woman is not a typical traveler. Salak was the first person to kayak 600 miles down the Niger River in West Africa. She was also the first woman to travel across Papua New Guinea. And she did these things alone.

Salak often takes risks to **challenge** herself. She also wants to learn how people live in the places she visits. From her travels and experience, Salak learned one **important** thing: "Challenges build **character** like nothing else. They teach you about yourself and others; they give you a deeper perspective[2] on life."

[1] If you **encounter** something or someone, you meet that object or person, usually unexpectedly.

[2] A **perspective** is a way of thinking about something.

Writer and explorer Kira Salak has traveled across some of the world's most extreme environments, including the Libyan desert.

# Free-Fall Skydiver

**Felix Baumgartner** is the world's fastest free-fall skydiver. In October 2012, the Austrian skydiver jumped from a balloon 24 miles (nearly 40 kilometers) above the Earth. His top **speed** was 833.9 mph (1,342 kph)— faster than the speed of sound.

Baumgartner was in danger the whole time. The air at a high altitude[3] is very cold and there is not **enough** oxygen.[4] Only Baumgartner's special suit **protected** him from these dangers. Why does Baumgartner take the risks? "I love a challenge," he says. "Trying to become the first person to break the speed of sound in free fall . . . is a challenge like no other."

▲ Skydiver Felix Baumgartner looks down on the Earth at the start of his long free-fall dive.

[3] **Altitude** is a measurement of height above the ocean.    [4] **Oxygen** is a gas in the air. All plants and animals need it to survive.

# Underwater Photographer

**Brian Skerry** is an underwater photojournalist. As part of his job, he encounters dangerous and mysterious sea creatures such as whales, sharks, and the huge Humboldt squid. To get the best photo, Skerry gets **close** to the wildlife—even if it's dangerous. One time in Mexico, a squid grabbed Skerry as he was taking a photo.

Why does Skerry take these risks? He **hopes** his photographs will make people think about life in the world's oceans. As Skerry says, "The oceans are in real **trouble**. . . . As a journalist, the most important thing I can do is to bring awareness."

While diving off New Zealand, Skerry and ▲ another diver had a close encounter with a southern right whale.

**A** | **Understanding the Gist.** Look back at your answer for exercise **D** question 3 on page 29. Were your predictions correct?

**B** | **Identifying Main Ideas.** What did each person in the reading do? Why does he or she take risks? Match the correct person (1–3) with each description (a–g).

> **1. Kira Salak      2. Felix Baumgartner      3. Brian Skerry**

_____ a. jumped from 24 miles above the Earth

_____ b. takes photographs of dangerous sea creatures

_____ c. was the first person to kayak down the Niger River

_____ d. was the first person to break the speed of sound in free fall

_____ e. was the first woman to travel alone across Papua New Guinea

_____ f. wants to learn how other people live

_____ g. wants people to care about the endangered oceans

**C** | **Critical Thinking: Synthesizing.** Think about the information in Reading **A** (pages 24–25) and the people in Reading **B** (pages 30–31). Answer the questions with a partner.

1. Reading A: "When people do something risky . . . this chemical [dopamine] creates a pleasant feeling." Which person in Reading B probably gets a pleasant feeling from taking a risk? _____

   How do you know this? _____

2. Reading A: "Some people take risks to achieve a goal." Which person or people in Reading B are taking a risk to achieve a goal? _____

   How do you know this? _____

**D** | **Critical Thinking: Reflecting.** Think about the risk takers in this unit. Discuss this question with a partner: Which person or people are most like you? Why?

☐ Daron Rahive      ☐ Michael Fay      ☐ Kira Salak      ☐ Felix Baumgartner

☐ Brian Skerry      ☐ Brady Barr      ☐ social risk taker      ☐ financial risk taker

☐ career risk taker                      ☐ other type of risk taker: _____

> **GOAL:** In this lesson, you are going to draft and edit sentences on the following topic:
> **What risks do you take? What risks don't you take?**

**A** | Read the information in the box.

---

**Language for Writing:** Negative Simple Present of *be* and Other Verbs

We use the simple present for habits, daily routines, facts, or things that are generally true. We use the negative form of the simple present to say what is **not** true.

To form the negative simple present with *be*, add *not* after *be*:

*I'm a skydiver. I **am not** a skier. / I**'m** not a skier.*

*Daron Rahive is a skier. He **is not** a skydiver. / He**'s** not a skydiver.*

*Skiing and skydiving are risky activities. Walking and dancing **are not** risky activities. / Walking and dancing **aren't** risky activities.*

To form the negative simple present with other verbs, add *do + not + verb*:

*I travel with other people. I **do not** (or **don't**) **travel** alone.*

*Daron Rahive feels in control in dangerous situations.*
*He **does not** (or **doesn't**) **feel** afraid.*

*Salak and Skerry take professional risks. They **do not** (or **don't**) **have** easy jobs.*

For more explanation and examples, see page 154.

---

Now complete each sentence (1–8) with the negative simple present form of the verb in parentheses.

**Example:** Risk takers ___don't like___ (*not like*) to be bored.

1. I _____ (*not go*) to parties alone.

2. Financi al risk takers _____ (*not be*) afraid to buy stocks.

3. The air at high altitudes _____ (*not have*) much oxygen.

4. Risk takers _____ (*not be*) nervous in dangerous situations.

5. Solo travelers _____ (*not feel*) lonely on trips.

6. Experts _____ (*not agree*) on how dopamine works.

7. A career risk taker _____ (*not be*) afraid to leave his or her job.

8. Some people _____ (*not like*) to work for others.

**B** | Rewrite the following affirmative statements (1–6). Change them to negative statements.

**Example:** Baumgartner avoids dangerous activities.

_Baumgartner doesn't avoid dangerous activities._

1. Kira Salak is a psychologist.

2. Most people enjoy dangerous activities.

3. Most of us are extreme athletes.

4. I take a lot of risks.

5. Brian Skerry works in the jungle.

6. The Humboldt squid is a small animal.

**C** | Write six sentences in your notebook using the negative simple present. Write about your daily activities. That is, what _don't_ you do?

**Example:** _I don't take the subway to school every day._

**D** | **Editing Practice.** Read the information in the box. Then find and correct one mistake in each of the sentences (1–5).

---

In sentences with the negative simple present, remember to:

- include the correct form of _be_: I **am** not; he / she / it **is** not; we / you / they **are** not.
- use the correct form of _do_: I / you / we / they **do** not; he / she / it **does** not.
- use the simple form of the verb after _do + not_. For example: I don't **like** _dangerous activities_.

---

1. I do not going skateboarding.

2. Most people does not like to take risks.

3. We not enjoy dangerous sports.

4. Kira Salak do not travel with a large group.

5. Good students do not to study for a test at the last minute.

**E** | Read the information in the box.

> ## Language for Writing: Adverbs of Frequency
>
> Adverbs of frequency say how often something happens.
>
>
>
> In sentences with *be*, put the adverbs of frequency after *be*. In sentences with other verbs, put the adverb before the verb.
>
> *I'm **never** late to class. I **always do** my homework on time.*
> *She**'s usually** careful with money. She **rarely buys** stocks.*
> *My children **aren't always** safe. They **sometimes do** dangerous activities.*
>
> **Note:** Do not use **not** with **never**: *We ~~don't~~ never play soccer without knee pads.*

Now put the adverbs of frequency in parentheses in the correct places in the sentences (1–6).

occasionally
V
**Example:** Teenagers drive too fast. (*occasionally*)

1. It's safe to skateboard without a helmet. (*never*)

2. Skydivers wear protective suits. (*almost always*)

3. Skerry meets dangerous sea creatures in his work. (*often*)

4. Surfing is dangerous. (*sometimes*)

5. I take chances with my money. (*rarely*)

6. Shy people talk to strangers at parties. (*hardly ever*)

**F** | How often do you do these activities (1–4)? Discuss your answers with a partner. Then write your answers using adverbs of frequency.

**Example:** A: Do you ever travel alone?  B: No, I never travel alone. ➝ *I never travel alone.*

1. travel alone: _____

2. speak in front of a large group: _____

3. talk to strangers at parties: _____

4. study for a test at the last minute: _____

**A** | **Brainstorming.** Brainstorm answers to the questions (1–3). Don't write complete sentences.

1. What are some common risks that people take? Make a list.

_____

_____

2. What kinds of risks do you take? Think of at least five examples.

_____

_____

3. What kinds of risks do you never take? Think of at least five examples.

_____

_____

**B** | **Planning.** Look at your ideas above. Circle three risks you take, and three risks you don't take.

**C** | **Draft 1.** Write three sentences in your notebook about risks you take and three sentences about risks you don't take. Use some adverbs of frequency in your sentences.

**Example:** I never travel in a car without wearing a seat belt.

**D** | **Editing Checklist.** Use the checklist to find errors in your first draft.

| Editing Checklist | Yes | No |
|---|---|---|
| 1. Are all the words spelled correctly? | | |
| 2. Is the first word of every sentence capitalized? | | |
| 3. Does every sentence end with the correct punctuation? | | |
| 4. Do your subjects and verbs agree? | | |
| 5. Did you use the negative simple present correctly? | | |
| 6. Did you use adverbs of frequency correctly? | | |

**E** | **Draft 2.** Now use what you learned from your Editing Checklist to write a second draft of your sentences. Make any other necessary changes.

# On the Move

## Think and Discuss

1. How do most people in your city get around?
   By car? By bicycle? By bus?

2. How many different ways of getting around a
   city can you think of?

◄ Cyclists move
through the traffic of
Shanghai, China,
after a light rain.

37

Look at the information on these two pages and answer the questions.

1. What do the graphs show?

2. Why do you think people in some countries drive alone a lot?

3. Why do you think people in some countries ride bikes a lot?

4. How often do you ride a bicycle or ride alone in a car?

5. Do you see your country or a country near you on the graphs? What are the percentages for that country? Is the information surprising?

# How often do you drive alone in a car?

**Percentage of Consumers in Each Country, 2012**

This graph shows how often people in different countries drive alone in cars or trucks. For example, in France, 56 percent of people drive alone every day or most days. In India, this number is 16 percent.

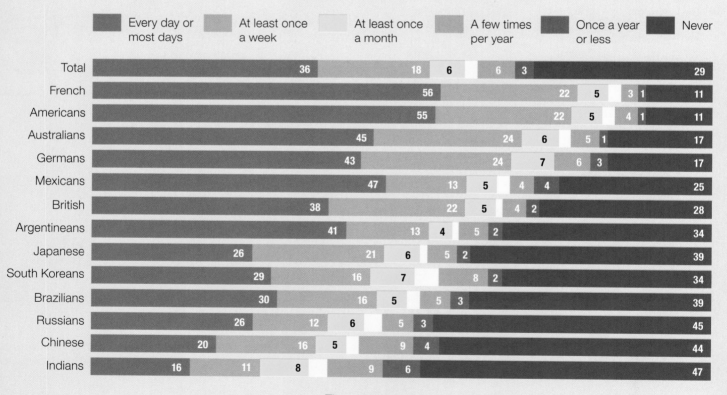

Every day or most days | At least once a week | At least once a month | A few times per year | Once a year or less | Never

| | Every day or most days | At least once a week | At least once a month | A few times per year | Once a year or less | Never |
|---|---|---|---|---|---|---|
| Total | 36 | 18 | 6 | 6 | 3 | 29 |
| French | 56 | 22 | 5 | 3 | 1 | 11 |
| Americans | 55 | 22 | 5 | 4 | 1 | 11 |
| Australians | 45 | 24 | 6 | 5 | 1 | 17 |
| Germans | 43 | 24 | 7 | 6 | 3 | 17 |
| Mexicans | 47 | 13 | 5 | 4 | 4 | 25 |
| British | 38 | 22 | 5 | 4 | 2 | 28 |
| Argentineans | 41 | 13 | 4 | 5 | 2 | 34 |
| Japanese | 26 | 21 | 6 | 5 | 2 | 39 |
| South Koreans | 29 | 16 | 7 | 8 | 2 | 34 |
| Brazilians | 30 | 16 | 5 | 5 | 3 | 39 |
| Russians | 26 | 12 | 6 | 5 | 3 | 45 |
| Chinese | 20 | 16 | 5 | 9 | 4 | 44 |
| Indians | 16 | 11 | 8 | 9 | 6 | 47 |

The white spaces in the graphs represent "Don't Know"/"Not Available."

# How often do you use a bicycle?

**Percentage of Consumers in Each Country, 2012**

This graph shows how often people around the world ride bicycles. In Australia, very few people ride bikes every day or most days. However, in China, 20 percent of the population rides a bicycle every day or most days. Only 16 percent of people in China never ride a bike.

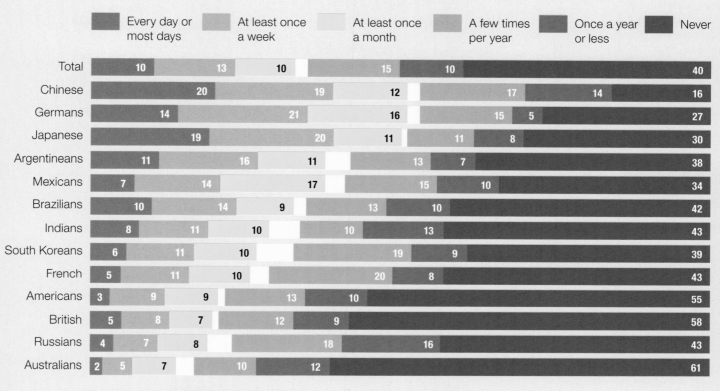

| | Every day or most days | At least once a week | At least once a month | A few times per year | Once a year or less | Never |
|---|---|---|---|---|---|---|
| Total | 10 | 13 | 10 | 15 | 10 | 40 |
| Chinese | 20 | 19 | 12 | 17 | 14 | 16 |
| Germans | 14 | 21 | 16 | 15 | 5 | 27 |
| Japanese | 19 | 20 | 11 | 11 | 8 | 30 |
| Argentineans | 11 | 16 | 11 | 13 | 7 | 38 |
| Mexicans | 7 | 14 | 17 | 15 | 10 | 34 |
| Brazilians | 10 | 14 | 9 | 13 | 10 | 42 |
| Indians | 8 | 11 | 10 | 10 | 13 | 43 |
| South Koreans | 6 | 11 | 10 | 19 | 9 | 39 |
| French | 5 | 11 | 10 | 20 | 8 | 43 |
| Americans | 3 | 9 | 9 | 13 | 10 | 55 |
| British | 5 | 8 | 7 | 12 | 9 | 58 |
| Russians | 4 | 7 | 8 | 18 | 16 | 43 |
| Australians | 2 | 5 | 7 | 10 | 12 | 61 |

Source: http://environment.nationalgeographic.com/environment/greendex/

▲ Cyclist and driver in a rain storm. Nairobi, Kenya.

**Word Partners**

Use **public** with nouns: public **transportation** (or public **transport**), public **park**, public **school**, public **good**, public **place**, public **speaking**, public **bikes**.

**A** | **Building Vocabulary.** Match the sentence parts (1–5 and a–e) to make definitions. Use a dictionary to check your answers.

1. _____ **Public** buildings and services

2. _____ If an amount or a number **rises**,

3. _____ To **carry** someone or something means

4. _____ A **crowded** place

5. _____ If a place or a thing is **comfortable**,

a. to take that person or object somewhere.
b. are for everyone to use.
c. is full of people.
d. it makes you feel good and relaxed.
e. it goes up in number, or increases.

**Word Partners**

Use **lose** with nouns: lose **weight**, lose **a game**, lose **your keys**, lose **your job**, lose **your memory**, lose **your hearing**, lose **your hair**.

**B** | **Building Vocabulary.** Complete each sentence (1–5) with the correct word or phrase from the box.

| behave | describe | health | lose weight | ride |

1. If you _____, you become less heavy.

2. A person with good health _____ will probably live a long time.

3. If you _____ something, you say what it is like.

4. The way that you _____ is the way that you do and say things.

5. When you _____ in a vehicle, such as a car, you travel in it.

**C** | **Using Vocabulary.** Answer the questions (1–4). Share your ideas with a partner.

1. Do you think it's OK to talk on a cell phone in a **public** place such as a bus or a train? Why, or why not?

2. What are some places in your town or city that are often **crowded**?

3. In what ways can public transportation be good or bad for your **health**?

4. What do some people do when they want to **lose weight**?

**D** | **Brainstorming.** List some types of public transportation in your country. Then list some good things and bad things about each one.

| Type of Public Transportation | Good Things | Bad Things |
|---|---|---|
| | | |

**Reading Skill:** *Previewing, Part 2*

In Unit 2, you learned that one way to **preview** a reading is to look at subheads and picture captions. Another way to preview is to read the first and last paragraphs of a reading passage. These two paragraphs may give you a clue about the main idea of the reading. They can also help you understand the details when you read the entire passage.

**A** | **Previewing.** Look at the photos and read the title of the reading passage on pages 42–43. Answer the questions.

1. What do you see in the pictures? _____

   _____

2. What do you think a "straphanger" is?

   A straphanger is someone who _____.

3. Now look at the subheads. Do you think the writer is going to describe mainly the good things or the bad things about public transportation? Which words in the title and the subheads give you a clue?

   _____

   _____

**B** | **Previewing.** Read the first paragraph on page 42 and the last paragraph on page 43. Then answer these questions.

1. Is your answer to question 3 in exercise **A** still the same?

2. Which words or phrases in the first and last paragraphs helped you decide your answer?

   _____

   _____

**C** | **Predicting.** Discuss the questions with a partner.

What do you think the passage on pages 42–43 is mainly about? What kinds of public transportation do you think you will read about?

_____

_____

# Rise of the Straphanger

track 1-06

**A** **TODAY, THERE ARE 600 MILLION** cars in the world. That may seem like a lot. However, there are over 7 billion people on our planet. Most of the world's population uses **public** transportation to get around. The number of people using public transportation continues to **rise**.

**B** Subway systems worldwide **carry** 155 million passengers each day. That's more than 30 times the number carried by all the world's airplanes. Every day in Tokyo, passengers take more than 40 million rides on public transportation.

**C** Yet many people see public transportation as "a depressing[1] experience," says author Taras Grescoe. They say it is slow, **crowded**, or too expensive. In fact, Grescoe says, it is actually "faster, more **comfortable**, and cheaper" than driving a car.

[1] Something that is **depressing** makes you feel sad.

## Better by Bus?

Like millions of people, Taras Grescoe is a "straphanger"[2]—a person who **rides** public transportation. In his book *Straphanger: Saving Our Cities and Ourselves from the Automobile*, Grescoe **describes** the benefits of public transportation. Firstly, it is better for the environment. When people use public transportation, they use less fuel. Twenty people on one bus use much less fuel than 20 people in 20 cars. Fewer cars means less pollution and cleaner air.

Using public transportation can be good for your **health** in other ways. It can even help you **lose weight**. In one study, a group of people took public transportation every day for six months. Each day they walked to a bus stop or a train station. In six months, each person lost an average of six pounds—almost three kilograms.

## Hope for Cities

Taking public transportation has another benefit, says Grescoe. It helps people become part of their community. When you are alone in your car, you don't talk to anyone. One Tokyo straphanger told Grescoe, "To use public transport is to know how to cooperate[3] with other people." It teaches you "how to **behave** in a public space."

So, public transportation is more than a way to get to work or school. It can help lead to cleaner cities. It may also lead to a healthier— and more cooperative—world population.

[2] The word **"straphanger"** comes from the straps people hold onto on trains or buses when they can't sit down.

[3] If you **cooperate** with someone, you work with them or help them.

The TransMilenio bus system in Bogotá, ▶ Colombia, works like an aboveground subway. The buses have their own lanes so they don't have to compete with cars. Some of the buses can carry up to 270 passengers.

A | **Understanding Purpose.** Look back at your answers for exercise **C** on page 41. Were your predictions correct?

B | **Identifying Key Details.** Complete the statements (1–5) with details from the reading passage on pages 42–43.

1. There are about _____ million cars in the world today.

2. Every day, _____ million people all over the world ride subway trains.

3. Some people think public transportation is _____,
   _____, and _____. But, says Grescoe,
   public transportation is _____, _____,
   and _____ than driving a car.

4. In one study, people lost weight after they took public transportation for _____
   months. They lost weight because they _____ to train stations and bus stops.

5. One Tokyo straphanger says public transportation teaches people how to _____
   with other people and _____ in public places.

C | **Critical Thinking: Guessing Meaning from Context.** Find and underline the following words in the reading on pages 42–43. Use the context to help you understand the meaning.

> **benefits** (paragraph D)    **fuel** (paragraph D)
> **pollution** (paragraph D)    **community** (paragraph F)

Now complete each definition with a word from the box. Check your answers in a dictionary.

1. A _____ is a group of people who live in a particular area.

2. _____ is something that you burn for heat or power,
   for example, coal or oil.

3. If something has _____, it has good results or it is helpful.

4. Dirty air from large cars is an example of _____.

D | **Critical Thinking: Analyzing Pros and Cons.** With a partner, complete the chart with information from the reading. Add any other pros and cons you can think of.

**CT Focus**

The **pros and cons** of something are its good points (advantages) and bad points (disadvantages). When you **analyze pros and cons**, you list the advantages and disadvantages to decide if it is a good or bad option.

| Pros of Public Transportation | Cons of Public Transportation |
| --- | --- |
| | |

Now read the last paragraph on page 43 again. Do you agree with the writer's opinion? Why, or why not?

# Crossing America

## Before Viewing

**A | Using a Dictionary.** Here are some words you will hear in the video.
Complete each definition with the correct word. Use your dictionary to help you.

| commuting | impact | innovations | revolution | steam | transcontinental |

1. _____ is the hot gas that forms when water boils.

2. _____ are creative new things or new ways of doing things.

3. _____ is traveling to work or school.

4. A _____ railroad is a train track that crosses from one side of a continent to the other.

5. If one thing has an _____ on another thing, it changes that other thing in some way.

6. A _____ is an important change.

**B | Thinking Ahead.** The video is about the history of public transportation in the United States.
What forms of transportation do you think you will see? Make a list with a partner.

## While Viewing

Read the items in the box. Listen and number them in order (1-6) as you watch the video.

| commercial airlines | steam trains | streetcars |
| steamboats | subway system | transcontinental railroad |

## After Viewing

**A |** Check your answers to the While Viewing exercise with a partner.

**B | Critical Thinking: Synthesizing.** Think about the information in the video, in the reading on pages 42–43,
and in the chartson pages 38–39. How do you think public transportation will change over the next 20 years?

◄ The completion of the
U.S. transcontinental
railroad, on May 10, 1869.

**A | Building Vocabulary.** Read the sentences below. Write each word in **bold** next to its definition (1–5).

Many cities have decided to improve their public transportation. Most people think this is a good **idea**.

Sometimes you have to wait at the bus stop for a long **period** of time.

Public transportation is great for people who don't know how to **drive** a car.

The **cost** of a subway ticket is low in most cities.

Many cities have **successful** subway systems. The trains work well, and people like them.

**Word Partners**

Use **idea** with adjectives: **good** idea, **bad** idea, **great** idea, **excellent** idea, **terrible** idea, **interesting** idea, **new** idea.

1. _____: to control the movement and direction of a car or a bus

2. _____: working well

3. _____: a thought or a plan

4. _____: the amount of money you need in order to buy, do, or make something

5. _____: a length of time

**B | Building Vocabulary.** Read the definitions below. Complete each sentence (1–5) with the correct word in **bold**.

If something is **easy**, it is not difficult or hard.

When you **spend** money, you pay for things that you want or need.

If you **earn** money, you receive money for work that you do.

A **problem** is something that causes difficulties, or that makes you worry.

You use *because* when you are giving the reason for something.

**Word Partners**

Use **spend** with nouns: spend **money**, spend **time**, spend **three hours**.

1. Traffic is a _____ in many busy cities. In some places, it can take more than an hour to travel ten miles.

2. Some people don't like public transportation _____ they think it is dirty and dangerous.

3. When you drive, it's _____ to get lost in a new city. You don't know the streets.

4. According to some studies, Americans _____ 18 percent of their income on transportation.

5. In a busy city, a taxi driver might _____ a lot of money in one night.

**C | Using Vocabulary.** Answer the questions (1–5) in complete sentences. Then share your answers with a partner.

1. Do your parents **drive** a car? Why, or why not?

   _____

2. What is the **cost** of a bus ride to the center of your city?

   _____

3. How much time do you **spend** traveling around every week?

   _____

4. What is one **problem** with public transportation in your city?

   _____

5. How do you get to class? Why do you use this form of transportation?
   Use *because* in your answer.

   _____

**D | Expanding Vocabulary.** Are the following words adjectives or nouns? Use a dictionary and check (✓) the correct column in the chart for each word.

| | adj. | n. |
|---|---|---|
| hopeful | | |
| cupful | | |
| beautiful | | |
| mouthful | | |
| handful | | |
| helpful | | |
| careful | | |
| useful | | |

| | adj. | n. |
|---|---|---|
| roomful | | |
| colorful | | |
| harmful | | |
| painful | | |
| thoughtful | | |
| thankful | | |
| trainful | | |
| spoonful | | |

**Word Link**

You can add **-ful** to some words to make adjectives. The suffix *-ful* means "full of." Sometimes words that end in *-ful* are adjectives such as *successful*. Sometimes they are nouns such as *houseful (of people)*.

Now write three sentences with three words from the chart.

1. _____

2. _____

3. _____

**E | Predicting.** Look at the title, subheads, and images in the reading on pages 48–49. Read the first and last paragraphs. What do you think the passage is mainly about?

a. a way to get more people to ride bikes in cities
b. the fastest way to travel across London
c. why bike riding is popular in China

# BIKE-SHARING  BOOM[1]

track 1-07

**A**    Big cities around the world are looking for ways to improve transportation. One way is bike sharing.

## What Is Bike Sharing?

**B**    The **idea** is simple. People pay a small fee[2] to use a bike for a certain **period** of time. For example, in London, you can ride around the city for an hour for just two pounds—about three American dollars. When you finish, you leave the bike at a docking station. Another person can then use the same bike.

## Why Is It a Good Thing?

**C**    Bike-share programs[3] are good for cities in several ways. Fewer people **drive** cars or ride on public transportation, so there is less air pollution. The streets are less crowded. The **cost** of starting a bike-share service is also less than building a new subway or bus system.

**D**    There are other benefits for the user. People don't have to buy and keep their own bikes. Instead, they can use public bikes whenever they need them. The cost to the user is low. In addition, cycling helps people stay healthy.

## Are There Any Problems?

**E**    Not all bike-share programs are **successful**. One problem is money. Janett Buettner is the author of a report on European bike-sharing programs. She explains, "The [bike-share service] operator[4] wants to earn money . . . [but] the user wants **easy** and cheap usage." The operator **spends** a lot of money to start the program. Many people have to use the program in order to pay for it. So, sometimes the operator does not **earn** a profit. When this happens, the program fails.

**F**    Some cities also don't have enough bike lanes. Paris, for example, is adding more than 160 miles (250 kilometers) of bike lanes to its streets. This adds to the cost of the program. In Paris and other cities, wet weather is also a **problem** for cyclists.

## What Is the Future for Bike Sharing?

**G**    Most bike-share programs will succeed, says Buettner, **because** they help to make cities "more livable." As London mayor[5] Boris Johnson says, cycling is "a clean, green, and healthy way to travel." That means it's good for the city—and its citizens.[6]

---

[1] A **boom** is a big rise in something.
[2] A **fee** is the amount of money you pay to be allowed to do something.
[3] A **program** is a service that helps with a social need.

[4] An **operator** is a person or a company that has a business.
[5] A **mayor** is in charge of the government of a city or town.
[6] The **citizens** of a town or a city are the people who live there.

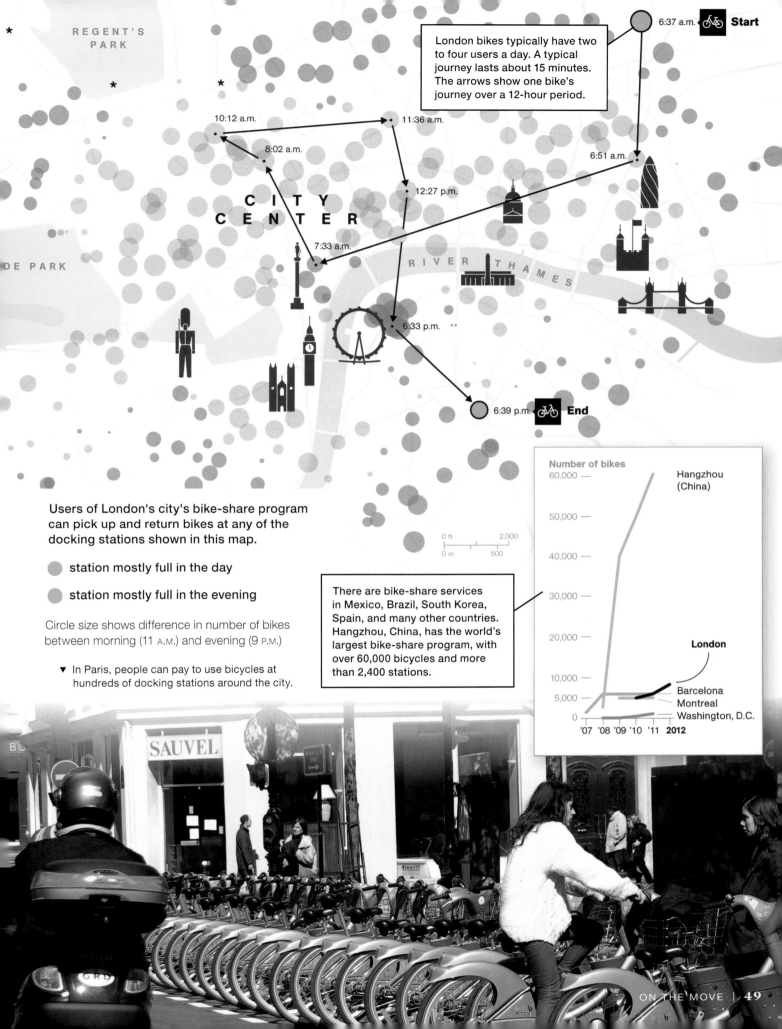

REGENT'S PARK

6:37 a.m. **Start**

London bikes typically have two to four users a day. A typical journey lasts about 15 minutes. The arrows show one bike's journey over a 12-hour period.

10:12 a.m.

11:36 a.m.

8:02 a.m.

6:51 a.m.

12:27 p.m.

C I T Y
C E N T E R

7:33 a.m.

R I V E R   T H A M E S

DE PARK

6:33 p.m.

6:39 p.m. **End**

Users of London's city's bike-share program can pick up and return bikes at any of the docking stations shown in this map.

● station mostly full in the day

● station mostly full in the evening

Circle size shows difference in number of bikes between morning (11 A.M.) and evening (9 P.M.)

▼ In Paris, people can pay to use bicycles at hundreds of docking stations around the city.

0 ft — 2,000
0 m — 500

There are bike-share services in Mexico, Brazil, South Korea, Spain, and many other countries. Hangzhou, China, has the world's largest bike-share program, with over 60,000 bicycles and more than 2,400 stations.

Number of bikes

60,000 — Hangzhou (China)

50,000 —

40,000 —

30,000 —

20,000 —

**London**

10,000 —

5,000 — Barcelona
Montreal
0 — Washington, D.C.

'07 '08 '09 '10 '11 **2012**

SAUVEL

**A** | **Understanding the Gist.** Look back at your answer for exercise **E** on page 47. Was your prediction correct?

**B** | **Summarizing Key Details.** Complete the concept map with information from the reading on pages 48–49.

**How does it work?**

- you pay _____ to use a bike for a period of time
- after using the bike, you leave it at _____

**Bike Sharing**

**Pros**

- **Good for cities**
  - fewer _____, so streets are less _____
  - less air _____
  - cost is less than a new _____ or _____

- **Good for users**
  - people don't have to buy and keep their _____
  - cost is _____
  - helps people to stay _____

**Future?**

- Buettner: most programs will succeed because cities become _____

**Cons**

- **Problems for operator**
  - starting costs can be high
  - not always possible to earn _____

- **Problems for cyclists**
  - may need new _____, e.g., in Paris
  - some cities have _____ weather

**C** | **Understanding Infographics.** Use the map and graph on page 49 to answer the questions.

1. Typically, how many people in London use one shared bike in a day? _____
2. When are the stations around the edge of the city mostly full? _____
3. What are three other cities that have bike-sharing programs? _____
4. Where is the largest bike-sharing program in the world? _____

**D** | **Critical Thinking: Analyzing Pros and Cons.** Do you think a bike-sharing program is a good idea for your city? Why, or why not? List the pros and cons. Then discuss your ideas with a partner.

**E** | **Critical Thinking: Synthesizing/Evaluating.** Discuss in a small group: You work for the mayor of a large city in your country. You have $10,000,000 to spend on public transportation. On which of the following will you spend the money? Check (✓) one. Share your reasons with another group.

☐ better roads          ☐ a new bike-share program          ☐ new subway lines

☐ a better bus service   ☐ another idea: _____

**GOAL:** In this lesson, you are going to draft and edit sentences on the following topic:
**Compare and contrast different forms of transportation.**

A | Read the information below.

## Language for Writing: Comparatives

We use comparative adjectives to compare two people, places, or things.

*Subway trains are **longer than** buses.*
*The Tokyo subway is **busier than** the New York City subway.*
*The Paris metro is **bigger than** the San Francisco underground system.*

To form most comparative adjectives, add -*er* to the adjective:

small → smaller      hard → harder      cheap → cheaper

Add -*r* when the adjective ends in -*e*:

nice → nicer      large → larger      late → later

For adjectives that end in a consonant + vowel + consonant, double the last consonant and add -*er*:

big → bigger      thin → thinner      hot → hotter

For two-syllable adjectives that end in -*y*, drop the -*y* and add -*ier*:

easy → easier      lucky → luckier      happy → happier

For most other two-syllable adjectives and adjectives with three or more syllables, use the word *more*:

successful → more successful      crowded → more crowded

Some adjectives have irregular comparative forms:

good → better      bad → worse      far → farther/further

For further explanation and more examples of comparatives, see page 156.

Now write the comparative form of each adjective.

| Adjective | Comparative Adjective | Adjective | Comparative Adjective |
| --- | --- | --- | --- |
| tall | | expensive | |
| busy | | cheap | |
| difficult | | big | |
| clean | | crowded | |
| dirty | | careful | |
| nice | | pretty | |
| good | | healthy | |

**B** | Combine each pair of sentences (1–4) to make one sentence with a comparative adjective.

**Example:** The subway is very comfortable. The bus is not very comfortable.

_The subway is more comfortable than the bus._

1. The subway station is very clean. The train station is not very clean.

_____

2. The bus station is very dirty. The train station is not very dirty.

_____

3. The A train is very crowded. The B train is not very crowded.

_____

4. Los Angeles is big. San Francisco is not very big.

_____

**C** | Write three sentences with comparative adjectives.

1. Cities _____ small towns.

2. I _____ my best friend.

3. (compare two places) _____

**D** | Read the information below.

### Language for Writing: Using because

We use *because* to give a reason for something. In the sentence below, the clause *because they help to make cities more livable* answers the question *Why will most bike-share programs succeed?*

      **main clause**           **adverb clause**
*Most bike-share programs will succeed because they help to make cities more livable.*

When we write a sentence with *because*, we use two clauses: a main clause and an adverb clause. A clause is a group of words with a subject and a verb. Some clauses are sentences, and some are not.

In the sentences below, *Ken takes the bus* is the main clause. It can also be a sentence by itself. The adverb clause is *because it is easy and cheap*. The subject of this clause is *it*, and the verb is *is*.

    **main clause**        **adverb clause**
*Ken takes the bus because it is easy and cheap.*

      **adverb clause**      **main clause**
*Because it is easy and cheap, Ken takes the bus.*

A clause that begins with *because* cannot be a sentence by itself. It must come before or after a main clause.

Now unscramble the words and phrases to make sentences (1–4) with *because*.

1. it / keeps me / I / ride my / healthy / bike everywhere / because /.

   _____

2. bought a new car / because / had many problems / We / the old car /.

   _____

3. subway system / because / I / like / easy to use / the New York / it's /.

   _____

4. a bike here / really busy / because / the streets / It's / hard to ride / are /.

   _____

**E** | Read the items (1–4). Connect the ideas in each pair of sentences with *because*.

1. **Fact:** My father takes the bus to work.
   **Reason:** He doesn't have a parking space at his office.

   _____

2. **Reason:** It's dangerous.
   **Fact:** I don't take the subway in my city.

   _____

3. **Fact:** My sister takes a train to class.
   **Reason:** It's faster than the bus.

   _____

4. **Reason:** My city doesn't have bike lanes.
   **Fact:** I never ride my bike to work.

   _____

**F** | Circle the word or phrase that makes the sentences (1–4) true for you. Then complete each sentence with a reason.

1. I **ride / don't ride** the bus a lot because _____.

2. I **like / don't like** public transportation because _____.

3. Because _____, I **drive / don't drive** to school.

4. Because _____, I **ride / don't ride** a bike.

**A | Brainstorming.** With a partner, add two forms of transportation to the chart. Brainstorm adjectives to describe each one. Write notes to complete the chart.

| | Walking | Bicycle | Car | _____ | _____ |
|---|---|---|---|---|---|
| **Pros** | free | cheap | | | |
| **Cons** | | | | | |

**B | Planning.** Circle the two forms of transportation in the chart above with the most adjectives. You will write about these two forms.

**C | Draft 1.** Write six sentences to compare two forms of transportation. Use the chart in exercise **A** to help you. Write three sentence with *because* and three sentences with comparative adjectives.

**Example:** I ride the bus because it's cheap.    I don't like the subway because it's dirty.

The bus is cheaper than the subway.    The subway is dirtier than the bus.

**D | Editing Checklist.** Use the checklist to find errors in your first draft.

| Editing Checklist | Yes | No |
|---|---|---|
| 1. Are all the words spelled correctly? | | |
| 2. Is the first word of every sentence capitalized? | | |
| 3. Does every sentence end with the correct punctuation? | | |
| 4. Do your subjects and verbs agree? | | |
| 5. Did you use comparative adjectives correctly? | | |
| 6. Did you use *because* correctly? | | |

**E | Draft 2.** Now use what you learned from your Editing Checklist to write a second draft of your sentences. Make any other necessary changes.

# Following a Dream

ACADEMIC PATHWAYS

Lesson A: Understanding main ideas and supporting ideas
Making inferences
Lesson B: Reading a biographical narrative
Lesson C: Writing sentences about the future

## Think and Discuss

1. What were some of your dreams for the future
   when you were a child? (For example, what job did
   you hope to have? What places did you want to visit?)
2. What are some of your dreams for the future now?
   Are they different?

▲ A team of explorers celebrates
reaching the North Pole.

## Exploring the Theme

Read the information and answer the questions.

1. What age group did Visa survey? What do those people dream of doing?

2. In the travel survey, which country did people from all regions plan to visit?

3. How do the survey results compare with your dreams and plans?

## Top Destinations

This chart shows the percentage of travelers from different regions who plan to visit certain countries in the next two years.

| People from . . . | Plan to visit . . . | |
|---|---|---|
| **Asia Pacific** | Japan | 30% |
| | United States | 21% |
| | United Kingdom | 20% |
| **the Americas** | United States | 34% |
| | United Kingdom | 26% |
| | Italy | 23% |
| **Europe, Middle East, and Africa** | Italy | 15% |
| | France, Spain | 14% |
| | United Kingdom | 13% |

Sources: www.visa.com.sg/aboutvisa/research/index.shtml
http://www.visa-asia.com/millennials/

▲ A group of trekkers is taking a rest to photograph Rinjani volcano, in Lombok, Indonesia.

# Dreaming Big

Were you born between 1982 and 1995? If so, you are part of "Gen Y." These people make up more than 25 percent of the world's population.

What are the dreams of Gen Y? In 2011, the company Visa asked Gen Y people in different countries about their dreams for the future. The results showed that young people worldwide share many of the same dreams. For example, many Gen Y people dream of having their own business, exploring other cultures, and traveling.

In another survey, Visa asked 11,620 adults around the world about their travel plans for the next two years. One of the top travel choices in 2011 was the United Kingdom. People also planned to visit Japan, Australia, the United States, and China. Visa also asked people about their dream destinations—places they hope to visit one day in the future. Japan was the top choice (7 percent), above the United States, Maldives, Italy, France, and Australia (4 percent each).

**A** | **Building Vocabulary.** Match the sentence parts (1–5 and a–e) to make definitions. Use a dictionary to check your answers.

_____ 1. If you **agree** to do something,

_____ 2. A **company**

_____ 3. When something such as an event **happens**,

_____ 4. **Knowledge**

_____ 5. When you **plan** to do something,

a. it occurs, or takes place, usually by chance.

b. you say that you will do it.

c. you think about it carefully before you do it.

d. is a business that makes money by selling products or services.

e. is information and understanding about a subject.

**B** | **Building Vocabulary.** Complete each sentence (1–5) with the correct word or phrase from the box.

| achieve | determined | interested in | practice | smart |

1. If you _____ a new skill every day, you will soon become good at it.

2. _____ people usually learn new things quickly.

3. If you work hard, you will _____ your goals.

4. Students who are _____ to be successful usually become successful.

5. When you are _____ a subject, it is more fun to study it.

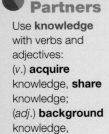

**Word Partners**

Use **knowledge** with verbs and adjectives:
(v.) **acquire** knowledge, **share** knowledge;
(adj.) **background** knowledge, **common** knowledge, **scientific** knowledge.

**C** | **Using Vocabulary.** Answer the questions (1–3). Share your ideas with a partner.

1. What countries or places do you **plan** to visit in the near future?

2. Which subjects do you have the most **knowledge** about?

3. What subject in school are you the most **interested in**?

**D** | **Previewing/Predicting.** Look at page 59. Read the title and subhead. Look at the picture and read the caption. Discuss this question with a partner:

*What do you think you need to do to become a pilot?*

Now look at the second page of the reading passage (page 60). Read the subheads and look at the picture and caption. Then answer these questions:

*What was Barrington Irving's dream? Did he achieve it?*

# REACHING FOR THE SKY

track 1-08

**A** In 2007, Barrington Irving became the youngest person to fly solo around the world. He was just 23 years old. How did this young man **achieve** this amazing feat?[1]

## A PASSION FOR FLYING

**B** A turning point[2] in Irving's life **happened** when he was 15. Irving was working in his parents' bookstore in Miami, Florida. One of the store's customers[3] was Gary Robinson, a professional pilot. One day, Robinson asked Irving if he was **interested in** flying. Irving didn't think he was **smart** enough. But the next day, the pilot took Irving to an airport. He showed Irving inside the cockpit[4] of a Boeing 777. That experience changed Irving's life.

**C** Irving was **determined** to fly. To reach his dream, he worked different jobs. He washed airplanes and cleaned swimming pools. He also helped at a store. At home, he **practiced** his flying skills on a video game. Finally, he earned enough money for flight school.

[1] A **feat** is a difficult achievement.
[2] A **turning point** is a time when an important change happens.
[3] **Customers** are people who buy things.
[4] The **cockpit** of a plane is the place where the pilot sits.

▲ Barrington Irving in front of his plane, *Inspiration*. "I like to do things people say I can't do," he says.

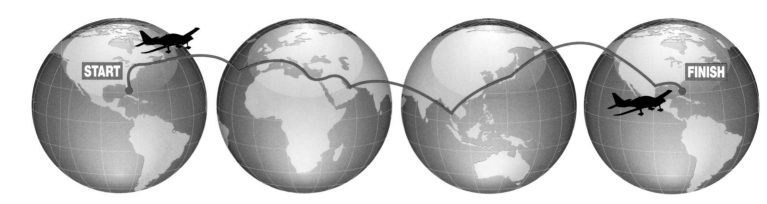

On his 26,800-mile (43,000-km) trip, Irving flew through monsoon[5] weather over India and sandstorms over the Middle East. In total, he flew across 13 different countries.

## CIRCLING THE WORLD

D  At flight school, Irving achieved his first dream—he learned how to fly. His next dream was bigger. He **planned** to build his own plane and fly solo around the world.

E  The first challenge was building the plane. Irving asked more than 50 **companies** for airplane parts. Most companies said no, but he kept asking. Three years later, he had parts worth $300,000. Columbia, an airplane company, **agreed** to build a plane using the parts. Irving named the plane "Inspiration."

F  On March 23, 2007, Irving began his round-the-world trip. After 97 days—with 145 hours in the air—he landed back in Miami. Irving had again achieved his dream.

## SHARING THE DREAM

G  When he landed, Irving saw many young people in the cheering crowd. This gave him an idea: "I had no money, but I was determined to give back with my time, **knowledge**, and experience." Irving decided to start a program called "Experience Aviation.[6]" The program helps young people achieve their career dreams in aviation and science.

H  "Everyone told me what I couldn't do," says Irving. "They said I was too young, that I didn't have enough money, experience, strength, or knowledge. [But] even if no one believes in your dream," he says, "you have to pursue it."

[5] The **monsoon** is a season of heavy rain in southern Asia.
[6] **Aviation** refers to the production and flying of airplanes and other aircraft.

**A** | **Understanding the Gist.** Look back at your answers for exercise **D** on page 58. Were your answers correct?

**B** | **Understanding a Sequence.** Put the events (a–h) in the correct order. Write the correct number (1–8) next to each event.

- [ ] a. Irving flew around the world.
- [ ] b. Irving learned to fly.
- [1] c. Irving met Gary Robinson.
- [ ] d. Irving asked over 50 companies for parts for his plane.
- [ ] e. Irving went to the airport and saw the inside of an airplane.
- [ ] f. Irving started a program to help young people achieve their dreams.
- [ ] g. Irving worked to go to flight school.
- [ ] h. Irving decided to build a plane and fly around the world.

**C** | **Identifying Key Details.** Read each statement. Circle **T** for *true* and **F** for *false*. Correct the false statements with a partner.

1. Irving was in his late twenties when he flew around the world.     **T**    **F**
2. Gary Robinson was a professional pilot.     **T**    **F**
3. Irving worked several jobs to earn money for flight school.     **T**    **F**
4. Irving used a video game to practice flying skills.     **T**    **F**
5. It took Irving five years to get the parts he needed to build a plane.     **T**    **F**
6. Irving flew around the world in 145 days.     **T**    **F**

**D** | **Critical Thinking: Guessing Meaning from Context.** Find and underline the following words in the reading on pages 59–60. Use the context to help you understand the meaning.

> **solo** (Paragraph A)    **parts** (Paragraph E)    **give back** (Paragraph G)    **pursue** (Paragraph H)

Write each word or phrase from the box next to its definition. Check your answers in a dictionary.

1. _____: to try to reach or achieve something
2. _____: to help others because people helped you
3. _____: pieces of a machine
4. _____: alone

**E** | **Critical Thinking: Making Inferences.** From the reading passage, we can infer that Irving has a strong character. Find and underline at least four sentences in the passage that show this.

> **CT Focus**
>
> **Inferring** means understanding something that the writer does not say directly. When you make inferences about a person, for example, you guess information about that person by the things he or she says and does.

**Reading Skill:** *Understanding Main Ideas and Supporting Ideas of Paragraphs*

The **main idea** of a paragraph is the most important thing, or idea, that the writer is saying. A paragraph usually has one main idea. This idea is usually, but not always, introduced in the first sentence of the paragraph. Other ideas in the paragraph support the main idea. These **supporting ideas** help to explain or give examples. They often answer questions a reader may have about the main idea such as *who, what, when, where,* and *how.*

track **1-09**

**A** | **Analyzing.** Read the paragraph. Check (✓) the main idea.

Jane Goodall had a childhood dream that came true. When she was young, she began reading books about animals and Africa. She decided that she wanted to go to Africa someday. Many years later, a friend told her about a man named Louis Leakey. Leakey was working in Africa, studying chimpanzees. Goodall met with Leakey. Leakey saw that Goodall had a great interest in animals, so he gave her a job. As a result, her childhood dream came true. Goodall has spent over 40 years working and studying chimpanzees in Africa.

☐ Jane Goodall read many books about Africa.

☐ Jane Goodall had a childhood dream that came true.

☐ Jane Goodall has worked in Africa for many years.

**B** | **Applying.** Find and underline supporting ideas in the paragraph above to answer the questions (1–3).

1. What did Goodall do to learn about Africa?

2. Who helped her achieve her dream?

3. How long has Goodall been working in Africa?

**C** | **Understanding Main and Supporting Ideas.** Read the three main ideas of paragraphs from the reading on pages 59–60. Write the correct paragraph letter (C, E, or G). Then complete the supporting ideas.

_____ **Main idea:** Irving wanted to help young people achieve their dreams.

 **Supporting idea:** He started a program called _____.

_____ **Main idea:** Irving built his own plane.

 **Supporting idea:** He asked companies for _____.

_____ **Main idea:** Irving did many different jobs to earn money for flight school.

 **Supporting idea:** He washed _____ and cleaned

 _____.

# Arctic Flyer

## Before Viewing

**A | Using a Dictionary.** Here are some words and phrases you will hear in the video. Complete each definition with the correct word or phrase. Use your dictionary to help you.

| break a record | endurance | land | persistent | stall | take off |
|---|---|---|---|---|---|

1. When you _____ in a plane, you leave the ground and start flying.

2. A _____ person always keeps trying.

3. When engines _____, they stop working.

4. When you _____ a plane, you fly it safely to the ground until it stops.

5. If you have _____, you are able to do a difficult activity for a long time.

6. If you _____, you do an activity better or faster than anyone else.

**B | Brainstorming.** Read the photo caption below. Discuss answers to this question with a partner: What difficulties do you think Gus McLeod experienced?

## While Viewing

Read questions 1–4. Think about the answers as you view the video.

1. How long in miles was Gus's flight?
2. What problem did Gus face after taking off?
3. Why wasn't Gus able to fly back to Maryland?
4. How do you think Gus felt at the end of his trip?

## After Viewing

**A |** Discuss your answers to the questions above (1–4) with a partner.

**B | Critical Thinking: Synthesizing.** Think about the lives of Barrington Irving and Gus McLeod. How were their dreams similar? How were they different? Whose achievement do you think was greater? Why?

Gus McLeod flew to ▶ the North Pole in this 1939 open-cockpit biplane.

N8NP

**A | Building Vocabulary.** Look at the **bold** words and phrases below. Use the context to guess their meanings. Circle the best definition for each word or phrase.

**Word Usage**

The word **graduate** is both a noun and a verb: If you **graduate** from college, you are a **graduate**.

1. If you are a **graduate** from a good college, it is usually easier to get a job.

   a. a person who has finished school or college    b. a person who is starting school or college

2. Gary Robinson decided to **invite** Irving to the airport the next day.

   a. ask to come                               b. ask for help

3. Some students work part-time so they can **afford to** go to school.

   a. have experience for                       b. have money for

4. Here is some **advice** that many successful people have: Never stop trying to achieve your goals.

   a. suggestion on what you should do          b. financial help

5. If you win a **prize** (such as money) in a writing contest, you are probably a very good writer.

   a. something you need to give to enter a competition
   b. something you get for doing well in a competition

**B | Building Vocabulary.** Complete the paragraph about a circus. Use the words in the box.

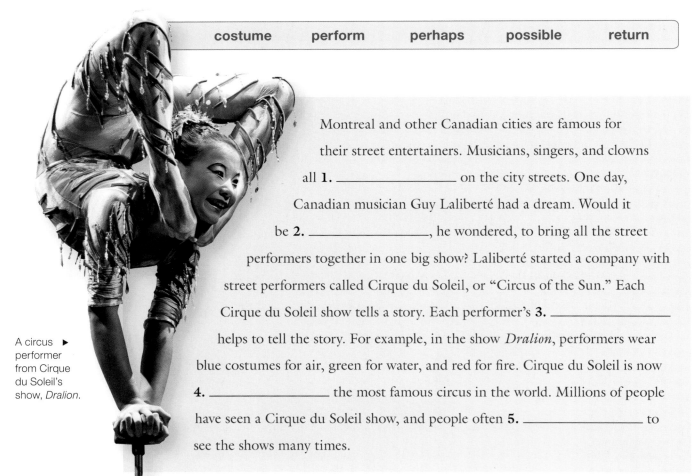

| costume | perform | perhaps | possible | return |

Montreal and other Canadian cities are famous for their street entertainers. Musicians, singers, and clowns all **1.** _____ on the city streets. One day, Canadian musician Guy Laliberté had a dream. Would it be **2.** _____, he wondered, to bring all the street performers together in one big show? Laliberté started a company with street performers called Cirque du Soleil, or "Circus of the Sun." Each Cirque du Soleil show tells a story. Each performer's **3.** _____ helps to tell the story. For example, in the show *Dralion*, performers wear blue costumes for air, green for water, and red for fire. Cirque du Soleil is now **4.** _____ the most famous circus in the world. Millions of people have seen a Cirque du Soleil show, and people often **5.** _____ to see the shows many times.

◄ A circus performer from Cirque du Soleil's show, *Dralion*.

**C** | **Using Vocabulary.** Answer the questions (1–4) in complete sentences. Then share your answers with a partner.

1. Have you ever won a **prize**? What did you win?

   _____

2. What place do you want to **return** to one day?

   _____

3. What do you hope to **afford to** buy someday?

   _____

4. When did you last wear a **costume**? What was the reason?

   _____

**D** | **Expanding Vocabulary.** Complete the sentences (1–5) with the correct verb and noun forms in the chart.

| Verb | | Noun | |
|------|------|------|------|
| achieve | invite | achievement | invitation |
| connect | perform | connection | performance |
| graduate | | graduation | |

1. Many people enjoy going to a concert to see a live music _____.

   They want to watch the musicians _____ on stage.

2. If you send an _____ to a party by email, you save paper,

   especially if you are going to _____ a lot of people.

3. Irving's _____ was flying solo around the world. Now, he

   wants to help other young people _____ their goals.

4. Cell phones help people _____ with others all over the

   world, even in places where there isn't a good Internet _____.

5. After they _____ from college, many students have

   _____ parties to celebrate with friends and family.

**E** | **Predicting.** Look at the title, captions, and photos in the reading on pages 66–67. Complete the sentence.

The reading is mainly about a person who achieved her dream of _____.

a. becoming an actress    b. winning a travel prize    c. working in a circus

# LIFE IN THE RING

track 1-10

**A** — **As a child,** Emily Ainsworth loved the colorful world of traveling circuses. As she grew older, she also became interested in other cultures. Above all, she wanted to travel. "England is a small country," she says. "I saved up for years . . . so that I could **afford to** fly abroad."

**B** — Ainsworth had many part-time jobs to pay for her travels, even working as a toilet cleaner. She also began to learn photography. When she was 16, she had enough money to travel to Mexico. The experience changed her life. She fell in love with Mexican culture and was determined to **return** one day.

**C** — As a 22-year-old anthropology **graduate**, Ainsworth got her chance. She won a BBC[1] contest called "Journey of a Lifetime." The **prize** of $4,000 went to the person with the most unusual adventure travel idea. Ainsworth's plan was to travel to Mexico to learn about the lives of circus workers. If **possible**, she wanted to become a circus worker herself.

**D** — Mexico has **perhaps** more circuses than any other country. One of the smaller, family-run circuses is the Circo Padilla. Soon after arriving in Mexico, Ainsworth met Padilla's ringmaster, Don Humberto. He **invited** her to visit his circus.

**E** — On her first day in Circo Padilla, one of the dancers could not **perform**. Don Humberto asked Ainsworth if she wanted to be a dancer. Five minutes later, Ainsworth says, she was in a dancer's **costume**. She stepped into the ring as "Princess Aurora." It was, she says, "like a childhood dream come true."

Emily Ainsworth took ▲ this photo of a young girl looking up at performers in one of Mexico's traveling circuses.

❝ When I was four,
I wanted to be
a trapeze artist. ❞

*Emily Ainsworth*

As a dancing circus princess, Ainsworth performed and lived with the other circus workers. As an anthropologist[2] and photographer, she studied and took pictures of circus life. Most days passed in a "sleepy haze,"[3] she says. But at night, the circus world came alive.

Ainsworth now has a career as a journalist[4] and photographer. Wherever she travels, she still feels a deep connection with Mexico and returns there often. "I still feel like a part of that world," she says.

Her **advice** to young people is to hold on to their childhood dreams. "When you're eight years old," she says, "you know that anything is possible."

▲ Emily Ainsworth with a circus performer in Mexico.

[1] The **BBC** (British Broadcasting Corporation) is a British TV, radio, and news organization.
[2] An **anthropologist** studies people, societies, and cultures.
[3] If you are in **a sleepy haze**, you are not thinking clearly because you have not had enough sleep.
[4] A **journalist** writes for a newspaper, magazine, or other media.

**A** | **Understanding the Gist.** Look back at your answer for exercise **E** on page 65. Was your prediction correct?

**B** | **Identifying Main Ideas.** Write the letter of the correct paragraph (A, B, C, E, F) from the reading on pages 66–67 next to its main idea.

_____ 1. Ainsworth won some money, so she was able to return to Mexico.

_____ 2. Ainsworth performed in the circus while she studied it.

_____ 3. Ainsworth had two early dreams: traveling and working in a circus.

_____ 4. Ainsworth's first trip to Mexico changed her life.

_____ 5. Ainsworth got a job in the circus because one of the dancers could not perform.

**C** | **Understanding Supporting Ideas.** Complete the supporting ideas with details from the reading. Which main idea does each one support? Write the correct paragraph letter from exercise **B** next to each supporting idea.

| Supporting Idea | Paragraph |
| --- | --- |
| 1. To save money to go to Mexico the first time, Ainsworth _____ _____. | _____ |
| 2. Ainsworth got money to go to Mexico again because she _____ _____. | _____ |
| 3. When she was not performing, Ainsworth _____ _____. | _____ |

**D** | **Critical Thinking: Making Inferences.** Discuss the questions (1–2) in a small group. Underline information on pages 66-67 that helps you answer each question.

1. How did Ainsworth feel about being a circus dancer?

2. How does Ainsworth feel about Mexico now?

**D** | **Critical Thinking: Synthesizing.** Discuss these questions in a small group:

1. In what ways are Barrington Irving and Emily Ainsworth similar?

2. Whose dream would you most like to follow? Why?

**GOAL:** In this lesson, you are going to draft and edit sentences on the following topic:
**Write about your dreams for the future.**

**A** | Read the information in the box.

---

**Language for Writing:** Using *plan*, *want*, and *hope*

You can talk about the future with *plan + to + verb*:

> Emily Ainsworth **plans to return** to Mexico someday.

Use *plan* when you are very sure something will happen.

You can also talk about the future with *want / hope + to + verb*:

> We **want to drive** across the Gobi Desert someday.
> She **hopes to have** enough money to travel someday.

Use *hope* and *want* to talk about things you want to happen, but you are not sure about.
You do not have a definite plan for these things yet.

---

Now complete the sentences (1–8) with the correct form of the verbs in the box.
Use each set of verbs only once.

| | | | |
|---|---|---|---|
| ~~hope / get~~ | plan / buy | plan / go | plan / graduate |
| want / eat | want / learn | hope / visit | want / walk |

1. Many college students _____*hope to get*_____ a good job after they graduate.

2. We _____ Spanish before we visit Spain.

3. My sister _____ to flying school because she wants to be a pilot.

4. Adventurous travelers often _____ new and unusual foods.

5. Most people aged 18 to 24 _____ a home someday.

6. I _____ the North Pole one day.

7. My brother _____ from college in three years.

8. Visitors to China usually _____ along the Great Wall.

**B** | Talk to your classmates and find someone who plans, wants, or hopes to do each of the activities in the chart. Then write sentences about four classmates.

| Activity | Name | Activity | Name |
|---|---|---|---|
| 1. make a lot of money | _____ | 6. try an extreme sport | _____ |
| 2. go to graduate school | _____ | 7. start a business | _____ |
| 3. perform in a play | _____ | 8. learn how to fly | _____ |
| 4. travel around Europe | _____ | 9. take a long vacation | _____ |
| 5. become famous | _____ | 10. design a house | _____ |

**Example:** **A:** Do you plan to travel around Europe?   **B:** Yes, I do.

Brad plans to travel around Europe.

**C** | **Editing Practice.** Read the information in the box. Then find and correct one mistake in each of the sentences (1–4).

> In sentences with *plan*, *want*, and *hope*, remember to:
> - use *to* + verb after *plan*, *want*, and *hope*.
> - use the base form of the verb (not *-s*, *-ed*, or *-ing*).

1. I plan get a job in France this summer.

2. Irving plans to helping young people who want to become pilots.

3. Some extreme athletes want breaking a world record.

4. Lara hope wears a beautiful costume in the dance performance.

**D** | Read the information below.

**Language for Writing:** Using Time Expressions

You can use general time expressions to talk about dreams and plans for the future:

*I plan to study Mandarin **someday**.*   *Sam hopes to return to Istanbul **in the future**.*
*We want to visit Dubai **one day**.*   *Marta plans to go to graduate school **in a few years**.*

You can also give specific times in the future:

*He hopes to go to flight school **in 2015** / **in five years** / **next year**.*

Time expressions appear at the end or at the beginning of sentences. When they appear at the beginning, put a comma after the time expression:

***One day**, we hope to see the Grand Canyon.*

Now use information from the chart to write three sentences about Lin's plans and dreams.

| Lin's plans | Next Summer | Next Year | In a Few Years | Someday |
|---|---|---|---|---|
| **Sure** | get a part-time job | visit Spain | graduate from college | learn to fly |
| **Not sure** | save some money | learn some Spanish | get a good job | live in Spain |

**Example:** _Lin plans to get a part-time job next summer._

_____

_____

_____

**E** | Look back at your chart from exercise **B**. Ask when each person plans, wants, or hopes to do each activity. Then rewrite your sentences in exercise **B** with a time expression.

**Example:  A:** Brad, when do you plan to travel around Europe?

**B:** Next summer

_Brad plans to travel around Europe next summer._

_Next summer, Brad plans to travel around Europe._

**F** | **Editing Practice.** Read the information in the box. Then find and correct one mistake in each of the sentences (1–4).

---

In sentences with time expressions, remember to:

- use the correct preposition and article (*a*, *the*) with **in the future**, **in a few years**, and **in [number] years**.
- use a comma when the time expression appears at the beginning of the sentence.

---

1. In a few years I hope to visit Mexico.

2. Many young people hope to own their own businesses on the future.

3. One day Rachel hopes to write a book about her adventures.

4. Most people aged 18 to 24 plan to buy a home in future.

**A** | **Brainstorming.** What are your plans and dreams for the future? Make a list with a partner. Write as many ideas as you can think of.

_____

_____

_____

_____

_____

**B** | **Planning.** Choose five of your ideas from exercise **A**. Label them *a*, *b*, *c*, *d*, and *e*. Write the letter of each idea in the appropriate place on the line below. Then add a time expression under each one (e.g., *in a few years*, *tomorrow*).

**Sure**
*(plan)*

**Not Sure**
*(want, hope)*

**C** | **Draft 1.** Use your ideas above to write five sentences about your dreams. Use *plan*, *hope*, and *want* and time expressions in your sentences.

**Example:**     I plan to become a doctor someday.

**D** | **Editing Checklist.** Use the checklist to find errors in your first draft.

| Editing Checklist | Yes | No |
|---|---|---|
| 1. Are all the words spelled correctly? | | |
| 2. Is the first word of every sentence capitalized? | | |
| 3. Does every sentence end with the correct punctuation? | | |
| 4. Do your subjects and verbs agree? | | |
| 5. Did you use *plan*, *hope*, and *want* correctly? | | |
| 6. Did you use time expressions correctly? | | |

**E** | **Draft 2.** Now use what you learned from your Editing Checklist to write a second draft of your sentences. Make any other necessary changes.

# The Information Age

## Think and Discuss

1. In what ways do you use the Internet?

2. What do you think the Internet is most useful for?

▲ Scientist and explorer Albert Lin uses the Internet and 3-D imaging to look for clues to an ancient mystery.

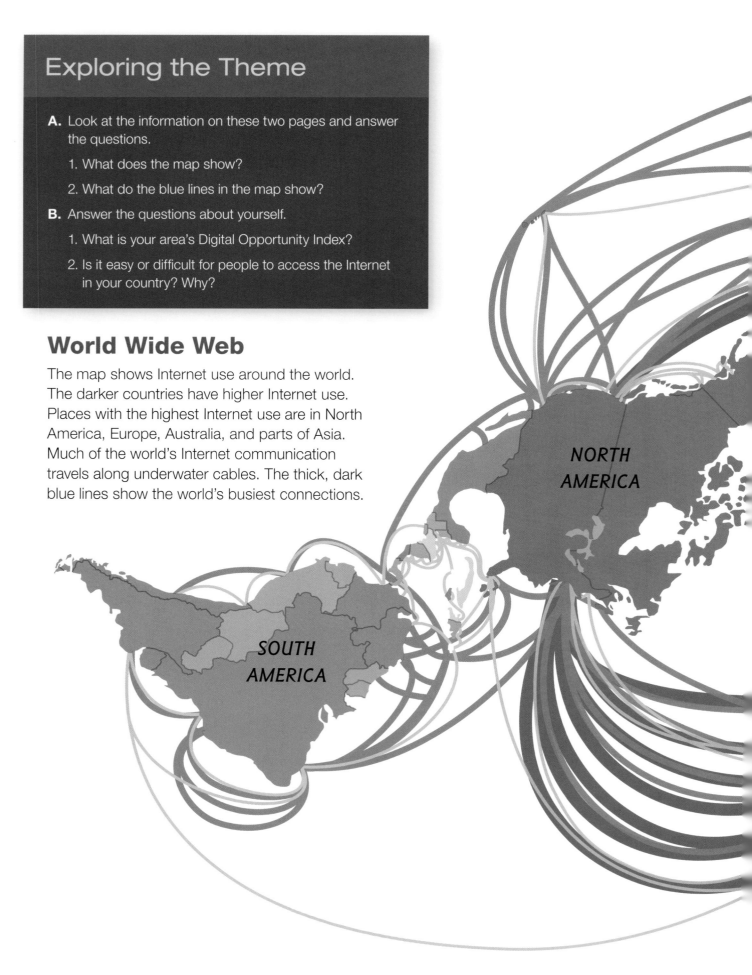

## Exploring the Theme

**A.** Look at the information on these two pages and answer the questions.

    1. What does the map show?

    2. What do the blue lines in the map show?

**B.** Answer the questions about yourself.

    1. What is your area's Digital Opportunity Index?

    2. Is it easy or difficult for people to access the Internet in your country? Why?

## World Wide Web

The map shows Internet use around the world. The darker countries have higher Internet use. Places with the highest Internet use are in North America, Europe, Australia, and parts of Asia. Much of the world's Internet communication travels along underwater cables. The thick, dark blue lines show the world's busiest connections.

NORTH AMERICA

SOUTH AMERICA

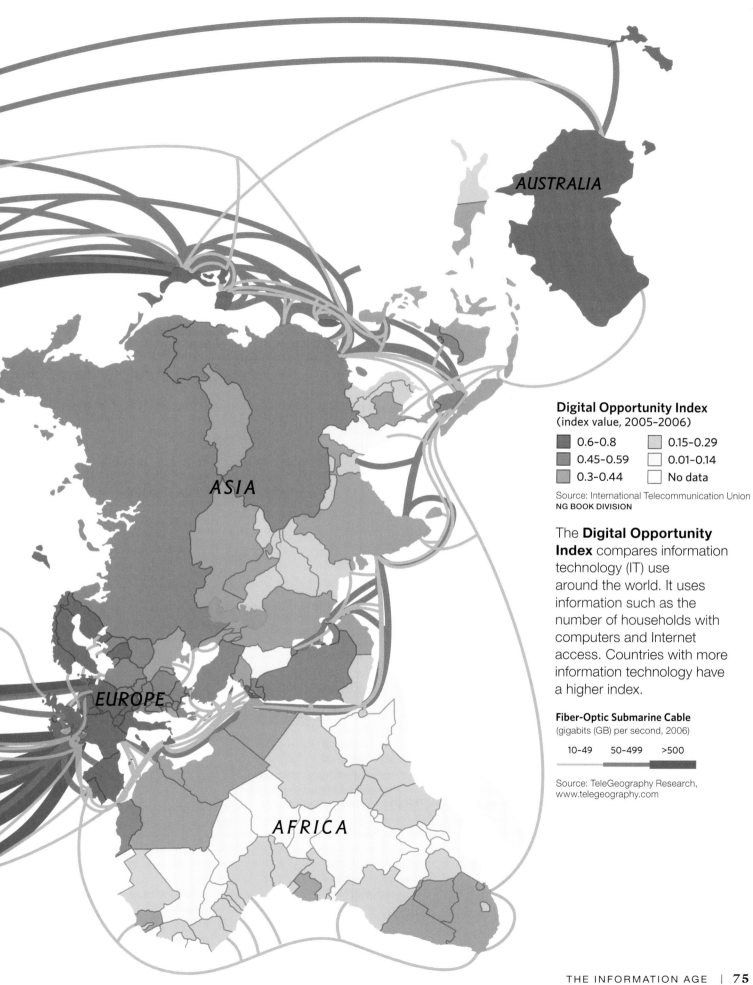

**AUSTRALIA**

**ASIA**

**EUROPE**

**AFRICA**

**Digital Opportunity Index**
(index value, 2005-2006)

- 0.6-0.8
- 0.45-0.59
- 0.3-0.44
- 0.15-0.29
- 0.01-0.14
- No data

Source: International Telecommunication Union
**NG BOOK DIVISION**

The **Digital Opportunity Index** compares information technology (IT) use around the world. It uses information such as the number of households with computers and Internet access. Countries with more information technology have a higher index.

**Fiber-Optic Submarine Cable**
(gigabits (GB) per second, 2006)

10-49    50-499    >500

Source: TeleGeography Research,
www.telegeography.com

**A | Building Vocabulary.** Read the definitions below. Use the words in **bold** to complete the sentences (1-5).

> Something that is **difficult** is not easy to do, understand, or deal with.
>
> Something that is **detailed** has a lot of small, individual parts.
>
> If something is **modern**, it is new or it relates to the present time.
>
> If something is **unusual**, it does not happen often or you do not see it or hear it often.
>
> A **clue** is a piece of information that helps you find an answer.

1. Beijing, China, has many old buildings and many _____ ones, too.
2. Reading information in another language can be very _____.
3. A person's name can sometimes be a _____ to their nationality.
4. The land in much of Mongolia is _____ because it is so flat.
5. Scientists need to make a _____ list of things they need for a research trip.

**B | Using Vocabulary.** Match the sentence parts below to make definitions. Use your dictionary.

**Word Link**

The suffix **-er** means "someone who does something." You can add it to some verbs to make nouns: lead**er**, climb**er**, teach**er**, own**er**, play**er**, work**er**.

| | |
|---|---|
| 1. ____ If something is **special**, it is | a. something that you cannot explain or understand. |
| 2. ____ A **mystery** is | b. the person who is in charge. |
| 3. ____ The **leader** of a group is | c. the end of a person's or an animal's life. |
| 4. ____ **Death** is | d. different or better than normal. |
| 5. ____ If something is **hidden**, it is | e. in a place where it cannot easily be seen or found. |

**C | Using Vocabulary.** Answer the questions (1-3). Share your ideas with a partner.

1. Can you think of any unsolved **mysteries**?
2. What places in the world are **difficult** to get to?
3. What **modern** buildings are in your area?

**D | Brainstorming.** List six things that people can do online. Share your ideas with a partner.

1. _use social networking sites_     4. _____
2. _____     5. _____
3. _____     6. _____

**E | Skimming/Predicting.** Skim the reading passage on pages 77–78 quickly. What do you think Albert Lin is trying to do?

a. find the tomb of a great leader     c. explore places no one has ever been to
b. ride across the whole of Mongolia

# In Search of Genghis Khan

track 2-01

**A** **EVERY DAY**, people use the Internet to share information. One special type of information sharing is called "crowdsourcing." When scientists or other people crowdsource, they ask a large number of people to help with a project.

**B** A team of scientists in the United States and Mongolia is using crowdsourcing to answer an 800-year-old mystery. The team is looking for the tomb of the Mongol leader Genghis Khan. At the time of his death in 1227, Genghis Khan ruled one of the largest empires[1] in history. But there are many mysteries about his life and death. One of the unanswered questions is: Where is Genghis Khan's tomb?

**C** Scientists believe Genghis Khan lies in a hidden grave[2] somewhere in the Burkhan Khaldun. This 7,500-square-mile area of Mongolia is difficult to get to. It is also too large to study on the ground. So the team uses satellite[3] images of the area. There are over 85,000 images, however, so the scientists need some help.

[3] An **empire** is a number of different nations controlled by one ruler.
[4] A **grave** is a place in the ground where a person's body is placed after they die.
[5] A **satellite** is a piece of equipment that is sent into space to receive and send back information.

◄ When we learn of an interesting site, says scientist Albert Lin, we "jump on horses or get in a helicopter and go check it out."

By the year 1227, Genghis Khan's empire stretched from East Asia to the Middle East.

D  More than 7,000 "citizen scientists" around the world are helping in the search. People help by logging on to a website. Then they label landmarks on very **detailed** satellite images of the area. The landmarks might be roads, rivers, **modern** structures, or old structures. They also label anything **unusual** as "other."

E  Humans can often do this kind of work better than computers, says project leader Albert Lin. "What a computer can't do is look for 'weird[4] things,'" he says. For example, a place labeled as "other" might be a **clue** to Genghis Khan's tomb. Lin's team uses this information to decide the best places to study.

F  How successful is the crowdsourcing project? Recently, the team found three interesting sites. One was a 3,000-year-old tomb. The second was a later tomb, but not Genghis Khan's. And the third site was a 13th-century Mongolian temple.[5] So far, Genghis Khan's tomb is still hidden. But Lin still hopes to find an answer to this great mystery of the past.

▲ Genghis Khan left a huge family when he died. Experts believe that one in every 200 men on Earth today is related to Genghis Khan.

[4] If something or someone is **weird**, they are strange or unusual.

[5] A **temple** is a building where people pray to their god or gods.

**A** | **Understanding the Gist.** Look back at your answer for exercise **E** on page 76. Was your prediction correct?

**B** | **Identifying Key Details.** Read each statement (1–5). Circle **T** for *true* and **F** for *false*. Correct the false statements with a partner.

| | |
|---|---|
| 1. Genghis Khan was born in 1227. | T    F |
| 2. Genghis Khan was the leader of the Mongol Empire. | T    F |
| 3. Scientists think Genghis Khan's tomb is in the Burkhan Khaldun. | T    F |
| 4. People worldwide are helping in the search for Genghis Khan's tomb. | T    F |
| 5. "Citizen scientists" are studying 7,000 satellite images. | T    F |

**C** | **Critical Thinking: Guessing Meaning from Context.** Look at this example from page 77.

*Every day, people use the Internet to share information. One special type of information sharing is called "crowdsourcing." When scientists or other people crowdsource, they ask a large number of people to help with a project.*

We can guess from the context—"Internet," "share," "information," and "help"—that, in this example, "crowdsourcing" means "sharing information on the Internet to get help from people."

Now find these words in the reading on pages 77–78. Use the context to guess their meanings. Then write each word next to its definition.

> **CT Focus**
>
> **Use context** —the words around a word—to guess the meaning of a new word. The context can also help you decide if the word is a noun, verb, or adjective.

> **tomb** (Paragraph B)     **logging on** (Paragraph D)     **label** (Paragraph D)     **site** (Paragraph F)

1. _____ : typing a username and password so you can use a computer or a website

2. _____ : a stone grave where the body of a dead person is placed

3. _____ : a place on which something is built

4. _____ : to put a name on something

**D** | **Critical Thinking: Evaluating Reasons.** Discuss these questions with a partner.

1. Why do you think Albert Lin and his team want to find Genghis Khan's tomb?

2. Why does Lin think humans are better than computers at finding possible clues?

**E** | **Personalizing.** Write answers to the questions.

Would you be interested in being a "citizen scientist" on this project?

Why, or why not?

**Reading Skill:** *Scanning for Key Details*

Sometimes you need to find important, or key, details quickly. To do this, you scan the reading. When you scan, you move your eyes quickly over the reading and look for specific things. For example, you can look for numbers to find times, dates, amounts, and distances. Capitalized words may be clues to names of people and places. Looking for nouns and verbs that appear several times may also help you find key details.

track 2-02

**A** | **Scanning for Key Details.** Read the questions below. Scan this paragraph for the answers to the questions.

**CT Focus**

**Use context** to guess the meaning of new words. What do *introduced*, and *stretched* mean?

> Genghis Khan was born around 1155. His birth name was Temujin. In his life, he achieved perhaps more than any other leader. At the age of 20, he brought armies together to fight for him. As leader of the Mongol Empire, he introduced a new alphabet and a new type of money. After his death, the Mongol empire grew to become one of the biggest of all time. It stretched east to west from the Sea of Japan to Eastern Europe, and north to south from Siberia to Southeast Asia.

1. When was Genghis Khan born? _____
2. What was his name when he was born? _____
3. At what age did he have armies to fight for him? _____
4. How far south did the Mongol empire reach? _____
5. How far west did the Mongol empire reach? _____

**B** | **Scanning for Key Details.** Scan the reading on pages 77–78 and answer the questions below.

1. How big is the Burkhan Khaldun? _____
2. How many images of Mongolia does the scientist team have? _____
3. What is the name of the leader of the scientist team? _____
4. How many people are helping the team? _____
5. How old is the temple that the team found? _____

▲ A stone tortoise stands on the site of Genghis Khan's capital city of Karakorum.

**Citizen Scientists**

◀ Scientists in Mongolia are searching for the tomb of Genghis Khan—with the help of "citizen scientists" around the world.

# Before Viewing

**A | Using a Dictionary.** Here are some words and phrases you will hear in the video. Complete each definition with the correct word or phrase. Use your dictionary to help you.

| indicator | man-made | out of the ordinary | tag |
|---|---|---|---|

1. _____ things are created by humans and are not natural.

2. If you _____ something, you mark it so someone can find it again.

3. If something is _____, it is unusual or special.

4. An _____ is a clue that helps us understand something.

**B | Thinking Ahead.** What kinds of challenges or difficulties do you think Albert Lin's team faces in Mongolia? Discuss your ideas with a partner.

# While Viewing

Read questions 1–4. Think about the answers as you view the video.

1. What is a good indicator that something is man-made?
2. How far is the site from the team's camp?
3. How does the team know that this is not Genghis Khan's tomb?
4. Why is the discovery of this tomb important?

# After Viewing

**A |** Discuss answers to the questions (1–4) above with a partner.

**B | Critical Thinking: Synthesizing.** Look back at the last paragraph on page 78. Which sentence probably describes the site shown in this video? How do you know?

**A** | **Building Vocabulary.** Read the definitions below. Use the words in **bold** to complete the sentences (1–5). Use a dictionary to check your answers.

> If you make a **discovery**, you find something for the first time.
> If things **spread**, they move out and reach a larger area or more people.
> You say that something is **amazing** when it is very surprising and you like it.
> A **contest** is a competition or a game.
> A **giant** animal or person is very large.

1. You can win prizes in a _____.

2. It is _____ to think that the Internet is less than 30 years old.

3. A popular video can _____ very quickly on the Internet. In one day, thousands of people can watch it.

4. Scientists made a surprising _____: Some 240,000-year-old dinosaur bones in Tanzania may be the oldest ever found.

5. *T. rex* was a _____ dinosaur. It was about six meters tall.

**B** | **Building Vocabulary.** Read the sentences below. Write each word in **bold** next to its definition (1–5). Use a dictionary to check your answers.

**Word Partners**

Use **direction** with adjectives:
**wrong** direction,
**right** direction,
**same** direction,
**different** direction.

> I think we're going in the wrong **direction**. We have to turn left here, not right.
> My laptop is **missing**. I left it on my desk but it's not here now!
> I'm going on **vacation** next month. I'll be in China for two weeks.
> While I was walking home in the rain, I saw a rainbow **appear** in the sky.
> All my classes are in the same **building**. They are in North Hall.

1. _____: a structure that has a roof and walls

2. _____: the general line that someone is moving or pointing in

3. _____: to begin to exist, or to be able to be seen

4. _____: a period of time when you relax and enjoy yourself, often away from home

5. _____: not in the usual place; possibly lost or gone

**C | Using Vocabulary.** Answer the questions (1-5) in complete sentences. Then share your answers with a partner.

1. Give an example of a **discovery** in the last 50 years.

   _____

   _____

2. Give an example of a photo or a video that **spread** quickly on the Internet.

   _____

   _____

3. What is the most **amazing** photo or video you ever saw online?

   _____

   _____

4. Do you take part in **contests**? If so, what kind? If not, why not?

   _____

   _____

5. What do you like to do on **vacation**?

   _____

   _____

> **Word Link**
>
> You can add **-ed** or **-ing** to some verbs to make adjectives. Adjectives ending in -ed usually describe feelings. Adjectives ending in -ing usually describe things that cause the feelings. For example: *I was **amazed**. It was **amazing**.*

**D | Expanding Vocabulary.** Complete the chart with the missing adjectives. Then write sentences using two pairs of adjectives.

| bored | boring |
|-------|--------|
| interested | |
| | amazing |
| | exciting |
| confused | |

1. _____

   _____

2. _____

   _____

**E | Predicting.** Look at the title and photos in the reading on pages 84–85. What do you think the reading is about?

a. photos of amazing animals that people shared online

b. how to take good vacation photos and share them online

c. how fake, or false, photos can spread on the Internet

track 2-03

**A** **FALSE, OR FAKE,** images are not new. In fact, the earliest fake photos date back to the 19th century. A famous example is the image below, called "The Cardiff Giant." The photo seems to show the discovery of a **giant** human. It was fake, but some people thought it was real.

**B** With computer technology, it is much easier now to make and share fake images. In 2004 another unusual photo **spread** around the world by email. Like the Cardiff Giant photo, it seemed to show the **discovery** of a very large human body. The photo usually came with a story under a title such as: "Giant Skeleton Unearthed!" Both the stories and the image were **amazing**. But there was a problem—none of it was true.

**C** The recent giant skeleton photo was the work of a Canadian illustrator. He made it for a digital art **contest**. The image was really a mix of three different photos. Making the image, says the illustrator, was not difficult. In fact, it took less than an hour and a half to create.

**D** So, how is it possible to tell if a photo is real? First, look for a source. Where does the photo come from? Is there a photographer's name? Look for clues in the photo. Sometimes the **direction** of light and shadows[1] is wrong. Is anything in the photo too big or too small, or is anything **missing**?

[1] A **shadow** is a dark shape on a surface. It forms when something blocks the light.

## Is it Real?

◄ News of a ten-foot-tall (three-meter-tall) human unearthed near Cardiff, New York, spread around the world in 1869. But the body wasn't real.

# Real or Fake?

E. The giant body photos seemed real to many people, but they were fake. Sometimes the opposite is true.

F. Dog owner Jason Neely took this amazing photo of his dog, Sidney, jumping to get a treat. "He's a crazy, crazy dog," says Neely. "He's constantly jumping like that." The photo later became part of a Photoshop contest. People created new, fake images on the Internet with Sidney jumping over signs, over **buildings**, even into space.

G. Melissa and Jackson Brandts took the photo below on **vacation** in Canada. They set their camera on a timer. By chance, a squirrel stood up just at the right time. The Brandtses sent their photo to *National Geographic*. Like Sidney, the squirrel became an Internet meme[2]—people used it to create fake images. The squirrel soon **appeared** in family photos, on the moon, even in a meeting with Barack Obama.

H. Digital[3] technology and the Internet are changing how we create and share images. But don't believe everything you see!

[2] A **meme** is an image, a video, or an idea that spreads from person to person by the Internet.
[3] **Digital** systems record or send information using thousands of very small signals.

A | **Understanding the Gist.** Look back at your answer for exercise **E** on page 83. Was your prediction correct?

B | **Identifying Key Details.** Put each description (a–h) in the correct place in the Venn diagram.

a. real
b. fake
c. vacation photo

d. spread by the Internet
e. made by an illustrator from Canada
f. other people created fake images with this photo

g. the animal's owner took the photo
h. seems to show a large human body

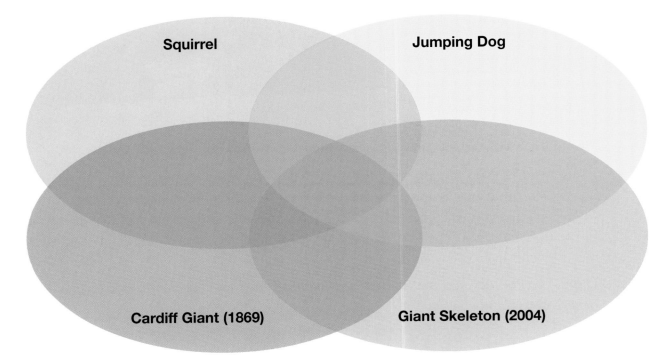

Squirrel

Jumping Dog

Cardiff Giant (1869)

Giant Skeleton (2004)

C | **Identifying Key Details.** Note answers to this question: What are three clues that can help you decide if a photo is real or fake?

_____

_____

_____

D | **Critical Thinking: Evaluating Reasons.** Discuss the questions (1–3) with a partner.

1. Why do you think people create fake photos?
2. Why do you think fake photos spread so quickly?
3. Why do you think Internet memes are so popular? For example, why did people create photos with the squirrel from the Brandtses' vacation photo?

E | **Critical Thinking: Synthesizing.** Discuss this topic in small groups. Describe the similarities and differences between the ways that people are using the Internet in the readings on pages 77–78 and 84–85, and the video.

**GOAL:** In this lesson, you are going to draft and edit sentences on the following topic: *How do you use information technology?*

A | Read the information below.

---

**Language for Writing:** Infinitives of Purpose

An infinitive is the base form of a verb starting with *to* (e.g., *to send*, *to share*, *to communicate*, *to find out*). We can use an infinitive of purpose when we want to say *why* we do something or *how* we use something.

How does Lin's team use the crowdsourced images?

> Lin's team uses the crowdsourced images **to decide** the best places to study.

Why do you use your car?

> I use my car **to go** out of town on the weekends.

Why do you exercise?

> I exercise **to stay** healthy.

You can also put the infinitive at the beginning of a sentence. Use a comma after the infinitive phrase.

How do you go out of town on the weekends?

> **To go** out of town on the weekends, I use my car.

How do you stay healthy?

> **To stay** healthy, I exercise.

---

Now match the sentence parts (1–3 and a–c) to make full sentences. Then rewrite each sentence with the infinitive phrase at the start.

| | |
|---|---|
| 1. I usually look for clues _____ | a. to get help finding Genghis Khan's tomb. |
| 2. Lin and his team ride horses _____ | b. to get around in Mongolia. |
| 3. Lin uses crowdsourcing _____ | c. to decide if a photo is fake. |

_____

_____

_____

**B** | Look at the example. Write a question for the other two answers in exercise **A**. Share your ideas with a partner.

**Example:** Why do you look for clues?

_____

_____

**C** | Write answers to the questions (1–2) using infinitives of purpose. Use your own ideas.

1. Why do most people use social networking?

_____

2. Why do you use email or texting?

_____

**D** | Read the information below.

**Language for Writing:** Using *and*, *but*, and *or*

You can connect ideas in a sentence with the conjunctions *and*, *but*, and *or*.
Use *and* to connect two or more items. You can also use *and* to connect two sentences.

With three or more items in a series, use commas to separate the items.
Use a comma to separate two sentences.

> I use Facebook **and** Twitter to share information.
> I use Facebook, Twitter, Instagram, **and** Pinterest to share information.
> I post on Facebook once a day, **and** I post on Pinterest once a week.

The conjunction *or* shows two or more choices. Use *or* to connect two or more items in a series or to connect two sentences.

With three or more items in a series, use commas to separate the items.
Use a comma to separate two sentences.

> Do you prefer Facebook **or** Instagram to post photos?
> I usually log on to Facebook, Twitter, **or** Reddit right after I wake up.
> I can send the photo by email, **or** I can post it on Facebook

The conjunction *but* shows two opposite or different ideas. Use *but* to connect two sentences.

Use a comma to separate the two sentences.

> I like Facebook, **but** I don't like Twitter.
> I never post on Pinterest, **but** I post a lot on Twitter.

Circle the correct conjunction in each sentence (1–8).

1. Every day I log on to Facebook, **and** / **but** I don't often use Twitter.

2. I use my laptop **and** / **or** my tablet—whichever is closest to my bed.

3. I leave for class at 8:00 A.M. I take the bus **but** / **or** drive my car.

4. When I ride the bus, I look at Facebook, send emails, **but** / **or** read on my tablet.

5. My tablet is useful, **but** / **or** I think it's quite heavy.

6. I have to take three buses to get to school—the 37, the 18, **or** / **and** the 5.

7. Sometimes I drive to school. Parking is expensive, **but** / **and** I like driving.

8. After class, I go to the library to do homework, **but** / **or** I go out with friends.

**E** | Write conjunctions to complete each sentence (1–6). Add commas where they are needed.

1. I post photos _____ videos a lot.

2. I read Buzzfeed Reddit _____ my local newspaper online every day.

3. To send email, I use my phone _____ my tablet.

4. Send me an email _____ a text when you get off work.

5. Do you want pizza sushi _____ hamburgers for dinner?

6. We can order pizza online _____ we'll have to wait a long time before it arrives.

**F** | Combine the sentences (1–6). Use conjunctions. Add commas where they are needed.

1. I use my laptop for work. I use my tablet for social networking.

   _____

2. Do you prefer Gmail? Do you prefer something else?

   _____

3. I usually take the bus to school. My neighbor drives me.

   _____

4. My neighbor comes over after class. We play video games.

   _____

5. My neighbor and I play Halo. We don't play Guitar Hero.

   _____

6. I post photos a lot. I don't post videos.

   _____

# WRITING TASK: Drafting and Editing

**A** | **Brainstorming.** Brainstorm answers to the questions (1–4). Use notes, not complete sentences. Share your ideas with a partner.

1. What kinds of information do you get from the Internet?

   _____

   _____

2. What kinds of information do you share on the Internet?

   _____

   _____

3. On a typical day, what information technology do you use?

   _____

   _____

4. What blogs or websites do you visit often?

   _____

   _____

**B** | **Planning.** Look at your ideas in exercise **A**. Choose five ways that you use information technology.

**C** | **Draft 1.** Use the information above to write five sentences about the ways you use information technology. Use some infinitives and conjunctions in your sentences.

   **Example:** I use an electronic dictionary to look up new words.

**D** | **Editing Checklist.** Use the checklist to find errors in your first draft.

| Editing Checklist | Yes | No |
|---|---|---|
| 1. Are all the words spelled correctly? | | |
| 2. Is the first word of every sentence capitalized? | | |
| 3. Does every sentence end with the correct punctuation? | | |
| 4. Do your subjects and verbs agree? | | |
| 5. Did you use infinitives correctly? | | |
| 6. Did you use conjunctions correctly? | | |

**E** | **Draft 2.** Use your Editing Checklist to write a second draft of your sentences. Make any other necessary changes.

# Saving the Wild

ACADEMIC PATHWAYS

## Think and Discuss

1. Which of the world's animals are disappearing?
   Why are they disappearing?

2. What can people do to help save animals in danger?

▲ Four-month-old Moanda, a lowland
gorilla, holds the hand of a human
caretaker in Mpassa Reserve,
Republic of the Congo.

# Exploring the Theme

Read the information below and answer the questions.
1. In what ways can human activities be dangerous for animals?
2. Which animal in the photos below is most in danger of dying out?
3. What kinds of information does the IUCN use to make its Red List?

# Animals in DANGER

Animal species in many parts of the world are in danger of becoming extinct. This means that they are at risk of dying out in the wild. For many species, the greatest danger is human activity. For example, people build on land where animals live and find food. As a result, species lose their homes, or habitats. In addition, human activity has an effect on global temperatures. These changes affect animals' homes and food sources. Melting ice, for example, destroys the habitats of polar bears.

The IUCN* Red List is a list of animal species that are in danger. The IUCN looks at how many of each species live in the wild. They also look at how the population is changing over time. The three highest levels of risk are **Vulnerable** (high risk).**Endangered** (very high risk), and **Critically Endangered** (extremely high risk).

\* International Union for the Conservation of Nature

## Vulnerable

**Polar bears** live in the Arctic. There are about 20,000 to 25,000 polar bears left in the wild.

## Endangered

**Chimpanzees** live in Equatorial Africa. Their population is falling fast, mainly because of habitat loss. Since the 1970s, the number of chimpanzees has fallen about 50 percent.

## Critically Endangered

There are only between 110 and 130 **Blue-throated Macaws** left in the forests of Bolivia.

▲ Red-and-green macaws flying over Madidi National Park, Bolivia

▲ The brightly colored feather of a male peacock.

**A** | **Building Vocabulary.** Read the definitions. Use the words in **bold** to complete the sentences (1–5).

> If you can **safely** do something, you can do it in a way that is not dangerous.
> To **prevent** something means to stop it from happening.
> If there is a **chance** of something happening, there is a possibility that it will happen.
> If you **adapt**, you change your ideas or behavior for a new situation.
> The **sex** of a person or an animal is whether they are male or female.

1. You can tell the _____ of some birds by the color of their feathers.
2. Birds can _____ build their nests in high trees, away from animals that might harm them.
3. One way to _____ the extinction of animals is to protect their habitats.
4. When there are clouds in the sky, there's often a _____ of rain.
5. The climate is changing, and some animals must _____ to this in order to stay alive.

**Word Partners**

Use **chance** with adjectives, nouns, and verbs: (*adj.*) **good** chance, **slight** chance; (*n.*) chance **of success**, chance **of survival**; (*v.*) **get a** chance, **give someone/ something a** chance, **have a** chance.

**B** | **Using Vocabulary.** Complete each sentence (1–5) with the correct word from the box.

| almost | destroy | effect | predict | tough |
| --- | --- | --- | --- | --- |

1. One _____ of climate change is the melting of ice in the Arctic.
2. Life is getting _____ for polar bears because their habitat is starting to disappear.
3. _____ all of the rhinoceroses in Indonesia are gone. There are fewer than 60 left.
4. When people move into a new area, they sometimes _____ animals' habitats.
5. Experts _____ that higher temperatures will cause sea levels to rise.

**C** | **Using Vocabulary.** Answer the questions (1–3). Share your ideas with a partner.

1. What is one **effect** of climate change that you have heard about?
2. What is one way an animal in your country has **adapted** to its environment?
3. What do you **predict** the weather will be like in 20 years?

**D** | **Brainstorming.** The number of sea turtles around the world is getting smaller. What might be causing this? Make a list of possible reasons.

**E** | **Predicting.** Look at the photos and read the title and captions on pages 95–96. Scan the passage for names of people and countries. Then complete the sentence.

I think the reading passage is about how _____ is helping

_____ in _____.

# Sea Turtles Feel the Heat

track 2-04

**A** **SEA TURTLES** are some of the oldest species in the world. The earliest sea turtles appeared over 200 million years ago. Today, however, sea turtles are in trouble. Their populations are getting smaller due to human activities and climate change.

**B** In Australia, conservationists[1] are studying the **effects** of climate change on sea turtles. They believe global warming may affect sea turtles in several ways. First, warming temperatures lead to rising sea levels. As sea levels rise, beach areas become flooded.[2] Sea turtles lay their eggs in the beach sand. Flooding can **destroy** sea turtle nests and the eggs inside them.

**C** Global warming also raises the temperature of sand around a sea turtle's nest. The temperature of the nest affects the **sex** of the turtle's eggs. Warmer temperatures (above 84 degrees Fahrenheit, or 29 degrees Celsius[3]) produce mostly females. Cooler temperatures produce more males. So, as global temperatures rise, more female babies will be born. Scientists **predict** that in 50 years **almost** all sea turtle babies in northern Australia will be female.

[1] **Conservationists** take care of the environment.
[2] If a place is **flooded**, there is a lot of water covering land that is usually dry.
[3] **Fahrenheit** (F) and **Celsius** (C) are two scales for measuring temperature.

▲ An endangered green sea turtle.

◀ Brazilian Mariana Fuentes became interested in sea turtles while studying at college. After graduating, she found work as a conservationist in Australia, home to the largest green sea turtle population in the world.

D   To survive these changes, sea turtles will need to **adapt**. But adapting is difficult because the environmental changes are happening quickly. In addition, sea turtles are more at risk from other dangers, especially ones related to human activities. For example, some populations are getting smaller because of predators[4] brought in by humans. As conservationist Mariana Fuentes says, "We can't be sure if sea turtles will adapt on their own." They may need our help to survive.

E   One of Fuentes's projects is at Turtle Camp, a beach in northern Australia. Here, Fuentes helps to protect turtles that are laying eggs. She works with a team of rangers[5] and researchers. Together, they **prevent** predators such as wild pigs and dogs from eating the turtles' eggs. Without the rangers' help, the turtles were losing up to 90 percent of their eggs. Now there are fewer predators, so the turtles can **safely** lay their eggs.

F   In the next few decades, sea turtles will face some **tough** challenges. With human help, says Fuentes, they will have a better **chance** to adapt and survive.

[4] **Predators** are animals that kill and eat other animals.
[5] **Rangers** take care of forests, beaches, or large parks.

Sea turtles make their ▶ nests on beaches. They lay their eggs and cover them with sand.

**A | Understanding the Gist.** Look back at your answer for exercise **E** on page 94. Was your prediction correct?

**B | Understanding the Main Ideas.** Write the letter of the correct paragraph (A–E) from the reading on pages 95–96 next to its main idea.

_____ 1. Sea turtles may need help to survive climate change and other dangers.

_____ 2. Fuentes helps to protect the areas where sea turtles lay their eggs.

_____ 3. Sea turtles are an old species, but they are now in trouble.

_____ 4. Warmer temperatures affect the sex of sea turtles.

_____ 5. Climate change is causing problems for sea turtles.

**C | Understanding Key Details.** Complete the notes with details from the reading on pages 95–96.

Sea turtles have been around for more than _____ years.

Predators such as _____ and _____ are dangerous for sea turtles.

The number of sea turtles is getting smaller due to _____ and _____.

**sea turtles**

Before Fuentes and her helpers started Turtle Camp, sea turtles were losing almost _____ percent of their eggs.

Sea turtles lay their eggs in nests in the _____.

**D | Critical Thinking: Analyzing Causes and Effects.** Find and underline information on pages 95-96 that describes two effects of climate change on sea turtles. Then complete the flow chart. Check your answers with a partner.

**CT Focus**

When you **analyze the cause or effect** of an event, you identify the reasons why it happened or its results. Ask yourself: Why did this event happen? What happened because of this event?

Higher temperatures

_____ → flooding destroys the _____ inside the turtles' _____.

warmer sand → warmer nests → Too many _____ are born.

**Reading Skill:** *Understanding Reasons*

**Reasons** are a kind of supporting information. Writers use reasons to support the main idea of a paragraph. Reasons tell you why something happened or why a person did something. Words such as *because* (*of*) and *since* introduce reasons.

**Because of** *human activity,* *many animal habitats are disappearing.*
      **reason**                              **result**

**Since** *people are farming on animals' land,* *many animals are losing their food sources.*
      **reason**                              **result**

*So* introduces a result. It follows a reason.

*Climate change is melting Arctic ice,* **so** *the polar bears' habitat is disappearing.*
      **reason**                              **result**

▲ **Endangered:**
Fewer than
2,500 adult giant
pandas are left
in the wild.

**A** | **Analyzing.** Read the paragraphs. Circle the words that introduce a reason or a result. Then answer the questions.

track **2-05**

**a**     Giant pandas became endangered because people began to farm in their habitats. Farming destroyed the pandas' main food source, bamboo. However, the Chinese government created special areas for the pandas to live in, so now they have a better chance of surviving.

1. Why did pandas become endangered?

_____

2. Why do they have a better chance of surviving now?

_____

**b**     Some people kill sea turtles for food. However, scientists have found that many sea turtles are dangerous for humans to eat. Since the turtles' habitat—the ocean—is polluted with toxins—poisons such as mercury and bacteria—their bodies are also polluted with these toxins. Because the turtles' bodies contain these toxins, many people get sick and even die from eating sea turtle meat.

1. Why can people get sick from eating sea turtles?

_____

2. Why are sea turtles' bodies polluted?

_____

**B** | **Applying.** Reread the following paragraphs in the reading on pages 95–96. Answer the questions. Then underline the information that gives you the answers.

Paragraph A: Why are sea turtle populations getting smaller?

_____

Paragraph D: Why is it difficult for sea turtles to adapt?

_____

# WONDERS *of* MADIDI

## Before Viewing

A tree frog hides from predators under a leaf in Madidi National Park, Bolivia. ▲

**A | Using a Dictionary** Here are some words and phrases you will hear in the video. Complete each definition (1–5) with the correct word or phrase. Use a dictionary to help you.

1. If you _____, you cause things to change in a good way.

2. A _____ is an insect.

3. If an object is _____ to something, it moves toward it.

4. A _____ is a wall that is built across a river.

5. If a group of people or things has _____, there are many different types of them.

> attracted
> bug
> dam
> diversity
> make a difference

**B | Brainstorming.** Imagine you are going into a rainforest. What might the weather be like? What might you see? What lives there? List your ideas with a partner.

## While Viewing

Read questions 1–4. Think about the answers as you view the video.

1. What are the only two ways to travel in Madidi National Park?

2. What is the Bolivian government going to build in the park?

3. What does a bug light do?

4. How many bug species does Sartore think there are?

## After Viewing

**A |** Discuss answers to the questions (1–4) above with a partner.

**B | Critical Thinking: Synthesizing.** Compare the threats to Australia's sea turtles with the threats to Madidi's macaws and insects. Which threats do humans cause? Which threats can we help to change? Discuss your ideas with a partner.

**A | Building Vocabulary.** Match the sentence parts (1–5 and a–e) to make definitions.
Use a dictionary to help you.

_____ 1. If you talk about **nature**,    a. you feel surprised or upset by something.

_____ 2. If you **care about** something,    b. you refer to animals, plants, and other living things.

_____ 3. You use a **camera**    c. you know what it means, or why or how it happens.

_____ 4. If you are **shocked**,    d. to take photographs or video.

_____ 5. If you **understand** something,    e. you think it is important, and you are interested in it.

**B Building Vocabulary.** Complete the paragraph with the words and phrases in the box.

| aware of | disappear | issue | publish | save |

Animal populations are decreasing around the world. This is an important

_____ that affects us all. Many species are about to _____

because of human activities. In Indonesia, for example, people cut down trees in

the forests where the Sumatran orangutan lives. As a result of this and other human

actions, there are only about 7,300 Sumatran orangutans left in the world. Is it

possible to _____ endangered animals such as the Sumatran orangutan?

Conservation organizations such as the World Wildlife Fund (WWF) think so. They

_____ pictures and stories about endangered animals on the

Internet. This helps make people _____ the problems.

They offer other solutions, too. In Indonesia, for example, the

WWF is working with the government to help stop paper

companies from cutting down trees in orangutan forests.

◄ **Critically Endangered:** A Sumatran
orangutan at the Gladys Porter Zoo
in Brownsville, Texas

**C** | **Using Vocabulary.** Answer the questions (1–3) in complete sentences. Then share your answers with a partner.

1. What environmental **issues** are in the news right now?

   _____

2. What environmental issue do you **care about** the most?

   _____

3. Which endangered species are you **aware of**?

   _____

**D** | **Expanding Vocabulary.** Complete the sentences (1–5) with the prepositions in the box. Use a dictionary to check your answers.

> **Word Usage**
>
> Some verbs combine with certain prepositions: care **about**, worry **about**, be aware **of**, be shocked **by**.

| about | for | in | to | with |
|-------|-----|-----|-----|------|

1. Many people started to **pay attention** _____ sea turtles when they heard about Mariana Fuentes's work.

2. If you **think** _____ the effects of climate change on animals, you realize they need our help.

3. Conservationists **believe** _____ taking care of the environment.

4. To **prepare** _____ her career as a conservationist, Fuentes studied at a university in Australia.

5. Many conservationists **agree** _____ Fuentes—we need to help some species survive.

**E** | **Brainstorming.** Discuss this question in a group: What are some ways to make people aware of the problem of endangered species? Write your ideas below.

write articles about the problem      _____

_____      _____

_____      _____

**F** | **Previewing/Predicting.** Look at the pictures and read the title and captions on pages 102–105. What is the reading about?

a. a scientist who studies animals that are in danger of disappearing

b. a photographer who takes pictures to help save endangered species

c. a conservationist who gives talks to help save endangered species

◄ "This veiled chameleon could see its own image in the camera lens," says photographer Joel Sartore. "He was interested in it for a few minutes."

# Animals in the Frame

track 2-06

**A**    **NATURE PHOTOGRAPHER** Joel Sartore is passionate about[1] endangered species. He uses his **camera** to make people **aware of** environmental problems. You can see some of Sartore's photos on these pages. They tell the stories of animals that may **disappear** unless we work fast to **save** them.

**B**    Sartore's latest project is called Photo Ark. The goal of the project is to make a photographic record of the world's biodiversity. As Sartore says, "For many of Earth's creatures, time is running out."[2]

[1] If you are **passionate about** something, you have very strong feelings about it.
[2] If you **run out of** something, you have no more of it left.

▲ Joel Sartore rests with monarch butterflies in the Sierra Chincua Reserve, Mexico, home to the world's largest monarch butterfly population. "The branches of the trees bend under the weight of all the butterflies" says Sartore. "When the sun comes out, they take to the skies and it looks like an orange storm."

Martha, believed to be the last passenger pigeon, died in Cincinnati Zoo on September 1, 1914. ▼

**Q** How did you become interested in saving endangered species?

**A** When I was a child, I read about Martha, the very last passenger pigeon. Martha died in 1914. I was **shocked**. In the past, there were 5 billion passenger pigeons—probably more than any other bird. But here was the last one, and there was no way to save it. How did we let this happen? I couldn't **understand** it. I still feel the same way. I want to prevent this from ever happening again.

**Q** How does photography help to save endangered species?

**A** Photography is the best way to show problems to the world. It gets people to **care about** the problems. It's not enough to just show pretty animals in a beautiful landscape. Now, we must show the threats to these animals as well. The good news is that there are many ways to **publish** stories and photographs on environmental **issues**. Self-publishing on the Web is one way to do this. Even nonprofessional photographers can help to make us aware of these problems.

▲ A brown bear catches a salmon in mid air above a waterfall at Brooks Falls, Alaska. "The bears here are famous for catching fish in this way," says Sartore. "They attract crowds of 30,000 visitors or more each summer. Everyone is hoping to get the perfect shot."

▲ Minnows appear to fly over Wyoming's Powder River. "These fish are actually in an aquarium next to the river," explains Sartore. "I wanted to show some of the small fish that live in the area. The fish are at risk from natural gas drilling nearby."

▲ Ruben, a three-month-old baby chimpanzee, smiles for the camera at Lowry Park Zoo in Florida. "Ruben's mother left him," says Sartore, "so human caregivers at the zoo are raising him. While I took the photo, his caregivers were gently holding him, comforting him. Baby primates are much like human children—they need a mother to hold on to, even if it's human."

▲ The beautiful eyes of a Malayan tiger shine in this portrait for the Photo Ark at the Omaha Zoo. "We tried photographing him on a big black background," Sartore says, "but he just tore it apart. He looked like he really enjoyed it, too!" Luckily for Sartore, the tiger didn't have a problem with white paper.

**A | Identifying Main Ideas.** Look back at your answer for exercise **F** on page 101. Was your prediction correct?

**B | Understanding Key Details.** Complete the sentences (1–6) with information from pages 102–103.

1. The purpose of Photo Ark is to record the world's _____.

2. Martha was the _____ passenger pigeon.

3. At one time, there were _____ passenger pigeons.

4. Martha died in the year _____.

5. Sartore says that photographers must not show only _____.

6. One way to tell stories about endangered species is to publish them on the _____.

**C | Identifying Key Details.** Match each animal from the reading (1–7) with the correct information (a–g).

1. The chameleon _____
2. The monarch butterflies _____
3. The passenger pigeon _____
4. The brown bear _____
5. The minnows _____
6. The chimpanzee _____
7. The tiger _____

a. is named "Ruben."
b. is extinct.
c. are in an aquarium.
d. catches fish.
e. tore up Sartore's black paper.
f. was interested in the camera.
g. are in Mexico.

**D | Understanding Reasons.** Complete the answers to the questions. Then underline the information in the passage that helped you.

1. Why is Sartore interested in saving endangered species?

   Because he _____.

2. Why does Sartore think that photography can help save endangered species?

   Because photography _____.

**E | Synthesizing.** Complete the Venn diagram to compare Mariana Fuentes and Joel Sartore.

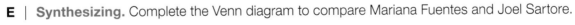

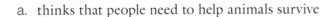

a. thinks that people need to help animals survive
b. helps by taking photos of many species
c. is recording hundreds of different species
d. mainly studies sea animals
e. works mainly in Australia
f. wants to make people aware of endangered animals

**GOAL:** In this lesson, you are going to draft and edit sentences on the following topic: *Write about an animal that is in danger. Why is it in danger? What will happen to it in the future?*

A | Read the information below.

**Language for Writing:** Giving Reasons

You can use *because* to introduce a reason:

> *Fuentes started Turtle Camp **because** she wanted to help sea turtles.*
> **result**                                            **reason**

You can use *so* to introduce a result:

> *Fuentes was worried about sea turtle eggs, **so** she got help from local rangers.*
> **reason**                                            **result**

Notice the comma in the sentence with *so*.

Now read the sentences (1–5). Label each sentence part *reason* or *result*.

1. Fuentes was interested in sea turtles, so she decided to help protect them.

   _____            _____

2. Australia is a good place to study sea turtles because it has a large sea turtle population.

   _____            _____

3. Fuentes works to protect animals in Australia because human activity is endangering them.

   _____            _____

4. Sartore was shocked by the story of Martha, so he decided to help endangered species.

   _____            _____

5. Sartore photographs endangered species because he wants to help save them.

   _____            _____

**B** | Complete the following sentences (1–5). Circle *because* or *so*.

1. The world population is increasing, **because** / **so** there are more cars on the road.

2. I want to help protect the environment **because** / **so** I take the bus every day.

3. Some sea animals are dying **because** / **so** the ocean is polluted.

4. It's easy to publish stories on the Internet, **because** / **so** we can all help make people aware of environmental problems.

5. Sartore created Photo Ark **because** / **so** he wanted to help save endangered species.

**C** | Combine the sentences (1–5). Use the words in parentheses.

**Example:** I care about air pollution. I take the subway to work. (*because*)
  *I take the subway to work because I care about air pollution.*

1. I take the bus to school every day. I want to save money. (so)

   _____

2. We recycle plastic. We don't want to pollute the oceans. (because)

   _____

3. We want to have cleaner air. Our city planted trees. (because)

   _____

4. I turn off the lights when I leave a room. I want to save electricity. (so)

   _____

5. We want to save trees. We use both sides of the paper. (because)

   _____

**D** | **Editing Practice.** Read the information in the box. Then find and correct one mistake in each of the sentences (1–4).

> **Editing for Language Mistakes**
>
> In sentences with *because* and *so*, remember to:
> - use *because* before a reason and *so* before a result.
> - use a comma in sentences with *so*.

1. Some animals cannot adapt to climate change so we need to help them.

2. Sartore publishes animal photos so he wants to help endangered species.

3. Fuentes wrote a book about an endangered species so she wanted people to learn about them.

4. The number of female sea turtles is rising so climate change is affecting turtle eggs.

**E** | Read the information below. Then unscramble the words and phrases to make sentences (1–3).

### Language for Writing: Speculating about the Future

When you talk about events in the future, you use *will* + base form of a verb.

    *Sea turtles **will survive** because Fuentes is helping them.*

If you aren't sure about something in the future, you can use certain adverbs to show that you are **speculating**, or guessing. These adverbs include *maybe*, *perhaps*, and *probably*.

    ***Maybe** Sartore will help people become more aware of environmental problems.*

    ***Perhaps** sea turtles will survive because of Fuentes's work.*

    *The World Wildlife Fund **will probably** help to save the Sumatran orangutan.*

*Maybe* and *perhaps* usually come at the beginning of a sentence. *Probably* comes after *will*.

**Example:**  the photos / people / maybe / will / endangered species / make / aware of / .

    *Maybe the photos will make people aware of endangered species.*

1. perhaps / rise a lot / in the next ten years / will / the sea level / .

    _____

2. the world population / by 2050 / will / be more than 8 billion / probably / .

    _____

3. governments / maybe / protect / will / the orangutans' habitat / .

    _____

**F** | Discuss these questions with a partner: How will the environment change in 10 or 20 years? What challenges will humans and animals face? Write three sentences about your predictions.

**G** | **Editing Practice.** Read the information in the box. Then find and correct one mistake in each of the sentences (1–3).

### Editing for Language Mistakes

In sentences with *will*, remember to:

- use the base form of the verb after *will*.

In sentences with adverbs for speculating, remember to:

- put the adverb in the correct position in the sentence. Put *maybe* and *perhaps* at the beginning of the sentence. Put *probably* after *will*.

1. I think sea turtles will probably having a better chance of surviving in the future.
2. Predators will stop probably eating turtle eggs.
3. Perhaps wild dogs will to be afraid to come to Turtle Beach now.

**A | Brainstorming.** Make a list of the endangered animals you read about in the unit. Add the names of endangered animals in your country, or others that you know about.

_____

_____

**B | Planning.** Choose the animal above that you are the most interested in. Then think about the answers to the questions below. Note information for each one.

1. Endangered animal: _____
2. Why are you interested in this animal?

   _____

3. Where does this animal live?

   _____

4. How many are left in the world?

   _____

5. Why is it endangered?

   _____

6. What do you think will happen to it in the future?

   _____

**C | Draft 1.** Use your notes above to write at least five sentences about the animal. Use *because* or *so*. Use speculation words if you are not sure about what will happen in the future.

**D | Editing Checklist.** Use the checklist to find errors in your first draft.

| Editing Checklist | Yes | No |
|---|---|---|
| 1. Are all the words spelled correctly? | | |
| 2. Is the first word of every sentence capitalized? | | |
| 3. Does every sentence end with the correct punctuation? | | |
| 4. Do your subjects and verbs agree? | | |
| 5. Did you use *because* and *so* correctly? | | |
| 6. Did you use *will* and speculation words correctly? | | |

**E | Draft 2.** Use your editing checklist to write a second draft of your sentences. Make any other necessary changes.

# Forgotten Heroes

## UNIT
# 7

ACADEMIC PATHWAYS

Lesson A: Understanding pronoun reference
Analyzing an argument
Lesson B: Understanding a historical account
Lesson C: Writing sentences to support an argument

## Think and Discuss

1. Make a list of items and devices that you use every day.
2. Do you know who invented these things?

▲ In the 2010 movie *1001 Inventions and the Library of Secrets*, actor Sir Ben Kingsley plays al-Jazari, a scientist who helped develop many items we use today.

111

# A World of Inventions

Every day, we see and use things that people invented in the past. Famous inventors created some of these items. For example, many people know that Thomas Edison invented the lightbulb. However, many inventors are not well known at all. Here are some examples of life-changing inventions with not-so-famous inventors.

## Signal Flare

In the early 19th century, American **Benjamin Franklin Coston** began developing a signal flare. After he died in 1848, his wife, **Martha Coston,** spent ten years completing the invention. She sold her signal flares to the U.S. government and all over Europe. Since the mid-19th century, signal flares have helped save lives all over the world.

## Exploring the Theme

# Helicopter

The world's first description of a flying machine appears in a fourth-century Chinese book called the *Baopuzi*. It had a spinning design like today's helicopters. In 1907, Frenchman **Paul Cornu** developed the Cornu Helicopter (pictured). His 20-second flight was the world's first helicopter flight with a pilot.

# Life Raft

Two inventors created early designs for a life raft: **Maria Beasley** and **Horace Carley**. Beasley created hers in 1882. Carley completed his in 1903. Their designs led to the life rafts found on today's boats and ships.

◄ A helicopter crew rescues a pilot floating in a life raft.

**Word Link**

Some nouns have the suffix *-ment*: move**ment**, entertain**ment**, argu**ment**, govern**ment**, employ**ment**, environ**ment**.

**A** | **Building Vocabulary.** Match the sentence parts (1–5 and a–e) to make definitions. Use a dictionary to help you.

1. _____ If you **invent** something,

2. _____ **Movement** is

3. _____ A **sequence** of events or things

4. _____ An **engineer** is a person who

5. _____ A **model**

a. designs or builds machines or structures such as roads and bridges.

b. a change in position, or going from one place to another.

c. is an object or a figure that shows what something looks like or how it works.

d. is the order in which they happen.

e. you are the first person to think of it or make it.

 **B** | **Building Vocabulary.** Complete each sentence (1–4) with the correct word(s) from the box.

| famous | history | include | machines | steps |
|---|---|---|---|---|

1. Inventing something involves several _____. For example, you have an idea, you build your invention, and then you test the invention several times.

2. Thomas Edison is one of the most _____ inventors in _____.

3. Edison's inventions _____ the lightbulb and the kinetoscope, a type of movie camera and projector.

4. Edison invented other _____, too, including an early electric train.

▲ A man looks into a kinetoscope, invented by Edison in 1889.

 **C** | **Using Vocabulary.** Answer the questions (1–3). Share your ideas with a partner.

1. Can you name any **famous** inventors? What did they **invent**?

2. Can you name a modern inventor? What did this person **invent**?

3. What do you think is one of the most important inventions in **history**? Explain.

**D** | **Predicting.** Look at the title, captions, and images on pages 115–116. What do you think the reading is mainly about?

a. an inventor from 800 years ago

b. the history of an 800-year-old invention

c. the steps inventors take to invent new things

# The Father of Engineering

🎧 track 2-07

**A** EIGHT HUNDRED YEARS AGO, a man in southern Turkey **invented** a remarkable[1] clock. It stood more than 23 feet (seven meters) high. At its base was a life-size **model** elephant. Inside the elephant was a water tank. Every half hour, the **movement** of a bowl in the water tank caused something amazing to happen. A **sequence** of sounds and movements began. Model birds, dragons,[2] and human figures started to move. The whole clock seemed to come alive. Then the bowl moved back, and the cycle began again.

**B** The clock's inventor was an **engineer** named al-Jazari. He lived in Diyarbakir, a city in southeastern Turkey. Al-Jazari was probably one of the greatest engineers in **history**. Some historians call him the "father of modern-day engineering."

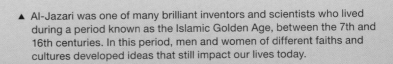

▲ Al-Jazari was one of many brilliant inventors and scientists who lived during a period known as the Islamic Golden Age, between the 7th and 16th centuries. In this period, men and women of different faiths and cultures developed ideas that still impact our lives today.

**C** We know about al-Jazari mostly from a book that he wrote. He called it the *Book of Knowledge of Ingenious[3] Mechanical Devices*. In many ways, al-Jazari's book is similar to the notebooks of the **famous** inventor Leonardo da Vinci. It describes **machines** of all shapes and sizes. They **include** clocks, hand-washing machines, and pumps[4] for lifting water. The book also has detailed drawings showing how each machine works.

[1] Someone or something that is **remarkable** is very unusual or surprising in a good way.
[2] In stories, a **dragon** is a large animal that has wings and breathes out fire.
[3] Something that is **ingenious** is very clever and involves new ideas, methods, or equipment.
[4] A **pump** is a machine that makes a liquid or a gas flow in a particular direction.

From this book, we know that al-Jazari was a great pioneer. In fact, many everyday items today—from toys to car engines—still use his ideas. Al-Jazari's machines with moving parts were some of the first **steps** toward modern-day robots.

D However, the machines were not just useful. They were also meaningful. In his elephant clock, al-Jazari used ideas from Egypt, China, Greece, and India. The clock did not just tell the time. It was also a celebration of different cultures.

E Today, it is still possible to see what al-Jazari's elephant clock looked like. A full-size working model stands in Dubai's Ibn Battuta Mall. There, every half hour, a bowl sinks, ropes pull, and mechanical figures begin to move. Al-Jazari's most amazing invention comes to life once again.

## How Does the Elephant Clock Work?

**1** A bowl with a small hole floats in a water tank inside the elephant's body.

**2** The sinking bowl pulls ropes that move a human figure. His moving pen shows the number of minutes past the hour.

**3** Every half hour, the full water bowl causes a ball to fall from the top of the clock. This causes a phoenix to move and make a sound.

**4** The ball drops out of a falcon's mouth into the mouth of a Chinese dragon. As the dragon moves around, it pulls the water bowl back up.

**5** Finally, the ball drops into a vase. The elephant driver moves and makes a sound, and the cycle begins again.

Al-Jazari's water-powered ▶ elephant clock celebrated influences from many different cultures, from Europe to China.

**A | Understanding the Gist.** Look back at your answer for exercise **D** on page 114. Was your prediction correct?

**B | Scanning for Key Details.** Complete the following sentences about the reading on pages 115–116. Note the paragraph where you find the information.

1. Al-Jazari lived in southern Turkey about _____ years ago. Paragraph: _____

2. Al-Jazari's inventions included _____ for lifting water. Paragraph: _____

3. Al-Jazari's inventions with moving parts were some of the first steps to today's

   _____. Paragraph: _____

4. Today, you can see an elephant clock in a mall in _____. Paragraph: _____

**C | Understanding a Process.** How does al-Jazari's elephant clock work? Number the steps (a–f) in the correct sequence.

a. The dragon pulls the bowl back up.

b. A ball falls and a phoenix makes a sound.

c. A bowl floats on the water in the tank.

d. The sequence starts again.

e. The bowl sinks and pulls on ropes.

f. The ball drops into a dragon's mouth.

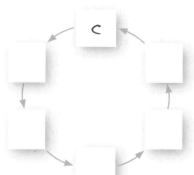

**D | Critical Thinking: Analyzing an Argument.** With a partner, complete the chart below about the reading on pages 115–116.

| | |
|---|---|
| What does the writer think of al-Jazari? For example, does the writer think he was an important inventor? | |
| Who does the writer compare al-Jazari to? How are the two people similar? | |
| What inventions and achievements does the writer include? How does the writer describe them? | |
| What words or phrases does the writer use to describe al-Jazari? | |

**CT Focus**

**Analyzing an argument** means looking at and understanding a writer's opinion or point of view. As you read, ask yourself two questions: *What is the writer's opinion about this topic? What evidence does the writer give to support this opinion?*

**Reading Skill:** *Understanding Pronoun Reference*

A **pronoun** is a word that stands for, or takes the place of, a noun. **Subject pronouns** are *I, he, she, it, you, we,* and *they.* **Object pronouns** are *me, him, her, it, you, us,* and *them.* A pronoun usually refers to a noun that comes earlier—in the same sentence or in a previous sentence.

To understand which noun a pronoun refers to, ask these questions about it:

- Is the pronoun singular (e.g., *he, she, it*) or plural (e.g., *they*)? The pronoun should match the number of an earlier noun.
- Is it a feminine pronoun (*she*), a masculine pronoun (*he*), or a gender-neutral pronoun (*it, they*)? The gender of the pronoun should match the gender of an earlier noun.
- Is the pronoun a subject pronoun or an object pronoun? Subject pronouns refer to subjects in sentences. Object pronouns refer to objects.

In the example below, the singular, masculine pronoun **he** refers to the man **al-Jazari**. The plural gender-neutral pronoun **they** refers to the plural noun **machines**.

> *A man named **al-Jazari** was one of the greatest inventors in history. **He** invented remarkable **machines**, and **they** were both beautiful and useful.*

**Matching Pronouns and Nouns.** Look at the **bold** pronouns in the paragraphs below.

Ask these questions about each pronoun:

- Is it a subject or an object pronoun?
- Is it a feminine, masculine, or gender-neutral pronoun?

Then draw an arrow to the noun that each pronoun refers to.

🎧 track **2-08**  We know about al-Jazari mostly from a book that **he** wrote. **He** called it the *Book of Knowledge of Ingenious Mechanical Devices.* In many ways, al-Jazari's book is similar to the notebooks of the famous inventor Leonardo da Vinci. **It** describes machines of all shapes and sizes. **They** include clocks, hand-washing machines, and pumps for lifting water. The book also has detailed drawings showing how each machine works.

From this book, we know that al-Jazari was a great pioneer. In fact, many everyday items today—from toys to car engines—still use his ideas. Al-Jazari's machines with moving parts were some of the first steps toward modern-day robots. However, the machines were not just useful. **They** were also meaningful. In his elephant clock, al-Jazari used ideas from Egypt, China, Greece, and India. The clock did not just tell the time. **It** was also a celebration of different cultures.

▲ An illustration from al-Jazari's *Book of Knowledge* shows one of the inventor's water-raising machines. The writing describes how the machine works.

# THE GOLDEN AGE

▲ Sir Ben Kingsley as the inventor al-Jazari, in a scene from the movie *1001 Inventions and the Library of Secrets*

## Before Viewing

**A | Using a Dictionary.** Here are some words you will hear in the video. Complete each definition with the correct word. Use your dictionary to help you.

| foundations | impact | ingenious |
|---|---|---|

1. The _____ of something are the things that it is based on.

2. Ideas are _____ if they are new and very clever.

3. If someone or something has an _____, they have a strong effect.

**B | Brainstorming.** You are going to watch part of a film called *1001 Inventions and the Library of Secrets*. In the film, a group of students is studying a period of history known as the Dark Ages. People usually use the term "Dark Ages" to describe Europe from about AD 500 to about AD 1200. Why do you think this period was called the Dark Ages? Discuss your ideas with a partner.

## While Viewing

Read questions 1–3. Think about the answers as you view the video.

1. At the start of the video, what impact do the students think the Dark Ages had on the modern world? How do they feel at the end of the video?

2. Why does the librarian/al-Jazari think we should call the period a Golden Age?

3. Which discoveries do the students learn about in the video? Circle the ones you hear or see.

| cameras | cinema/movies | computers | airplanes | helicopters |
|---|---|---|---|---|
| clocks | trains | televisions | cars | cell phones |

## After Viewing

**A |** Discuss the answers to the questions (1–3) above with a partner.

**B | Synthesizing.** Compare the information in the reading on pages 115–116 and the information in the video. Write answers to the questions.

1. What information is mentioned in both places? _____

2. What new information did you learn about al-Jazari in the video? Note two things:

_____   _____

**A | Building Vocabulary.** Read the sentences below. Write each word in **bold** next to its definition (1–5).

> Personal computers made a **huge** difference to the way people work. Many tasks are much easier now than they were before.
>
> Many people worldwide **recognize** the achievements of computer pioneers such as Steve Jobs.
>
> If you get a PhD in science, you may be able to have a career as a science **professor**.
>
> Fifty years ago, students had to do math with a pencil and paper. Now, they often use cell phones to **calculate** numbers.
>
> In most universities, a student has to write a **report** on a computer, not on paper.

1. _____: a written work that gives information about a particular topic

2. _____: to respect or show approval of something good

3. _____: very large

4. _____: add, subtract, multiply, or divide numbers

5. _____: a teacher at a university or a college

**B | Building Vocabulary.** Read the definitions below. Then complete each sentence (1–5) with the correct form of each word or phrase.

**Word Partners**

Use **reason** with adjectives:
**main** reason,
**only** reason,
**same** reason,
**simple** reason,
**good** reason.

> When children **grow up**, they get older and become adults.
>
> To **regard** someone in a certain way means to think of the person in that way.
>
> A **reason** for something is a fact or a situation that explains why it happens.
>
> The **aim** of something is the the purpose for doing it.
>
> If you **inspire** someone, you give that person new ideas and a strong feeling of enthusiasm.

1. Many people _____ Bill Gates, one of the founders of Microsoft, as the father of home computing.

2. Gates _____ and went to school in Seattle, Washington.

3. When Bill Gates was 13, he stopped going to his math class so he could work with a new computer. His _____ was to be able to write his own computer programs.

4. Gates's work led to the invention of modern-day computers, such as laptops. One _____ laptops are so popular is that you can take them with you wherever you go.

5. The stories of pioneers like Bill Gates _____ a lot of young people to be creative and follow their dreams.

**C | Using Vocabulary.** Answer the questions (1–4) in complete sentences. Then share your sentences with a partner.

1. Where did you **grow up**?

   _____

2. What job would you like to have? What is one **reason** you want that job?

   _____

   _____

3. Name two people who **inspire** you.

   _____

   _____

4. If someone does something amazing, what are two ways that people can **recognize** that person's achievement?

   _____

   _____

**D | Expanding Vocabulary.** Complete each sentence (1–8) with a phrasal verb from the box. Use a dictionary to help you.

| | | | |
|---|---|---|---|
| come up | come up with | give up | keep up |
| look up | save up | speak up | use up |

1. I need to _____ a word in the dictionary.

2. My mother doesn't spend a lot of money on clothes and shoes. She wants to _____ to buy a car.

3. Don't _____ the battery. I need to make a phone call.

4. I _____. I can't finish this book. It's too difficult to understand.

5. You walk so fast, and I can't _____. Can you please slow down?

6. Please _____. I can't hear you.

7. We didn't talk about the new project. The topic didn't _____ in our conversation.

8. Inventors _____ new and better ways to do things.

**E | Predicting.** Look at the title, captions, and images in the reading on pages 122–123. Read the first and last paragraphs. What do you think the passage is mainly about?

a. the story of a female doctor in the mid-19th century

b. holidays that celebrate scientists and mathematicians

c. the achievements of a female mathematician and scientist

> **Word Partners**
>
> A **phrasal verb** is made of a verb + a preposition or an adverb (or two prepositions or adverbs). The preposition or adverb can change the verb's usual meaning. For example, in the phrasal verb *grow up*, the verb *grow* does not mean simply *"to become larger."* Instead, *grow up* means *"to change from being a child to being an adult."*

# The Mother of COMPUTING

▲ Portrait of the 19th century mathematician Ada Lovelace, by Alfred Edward Chalon.

track 2-09

**A** **EVERY YEAR** on October 16, people celebrate Ada Lovelace Day. Today, Ada Lovelace is a role model for many young women. But who is Ada Lovelace and what is she famous for?

**B** When people think of computing pioneers, they usually think of men such as Bill Gates and Steve Jobs. These men made **huge** advances[1] in computer science. But historians believe the world's first computer programmer was a woman: Lady Augusta Ada King, also known as Ada Lovelace.

**C** Ada Lovelace was born in 1815 and **grew up** in London, England. Her mother was a mathematician and her father was the famous poet Lord Byron. As a young girl, she excelled[2] in her math and science studies. At the age of 13, she even created a design for a flying machine.

[1] An **advance** in a subject or an activity is progress in understanding it.
[2] If someone **excels** in or at something, they are very good at it.

**D** When she was 17 years old, Lovelace met a math **professor** named Charles Babbage. They became friends and enjoyed sharing their ideas about math. At the time, Babbage was working on a new **calculating** machine. He called it an analytical engine. Lovelace was very interested in his invention.

**E** In 1843, Lovelace translated³ a **report** on the analytical engine from French into English. She added her ideas and notes to the report. These included notes for a step-by-step calculation called an algorithm. Mathematicians today **regard** these notes as the first ever computer program.

**F** Ada Lovelace was one of very few female mathematicians and scientists in her time. Today, there are more women studying math and science than ever before, but they are still a minority. One **reason** may be that most math and science role models are men. The **aim** of Ada Lovelace Day is to **recognize** the achievements of women in science, engineering, and mathematics.⁴ In this way, Ada Lovelace continues to **inspire** girls and women to follow in her footsteps.

³ If you **translate** something, you say or write it in another language.
⁴ **Mathematics**, or math, is the study of numbers, quantities, or shapes.

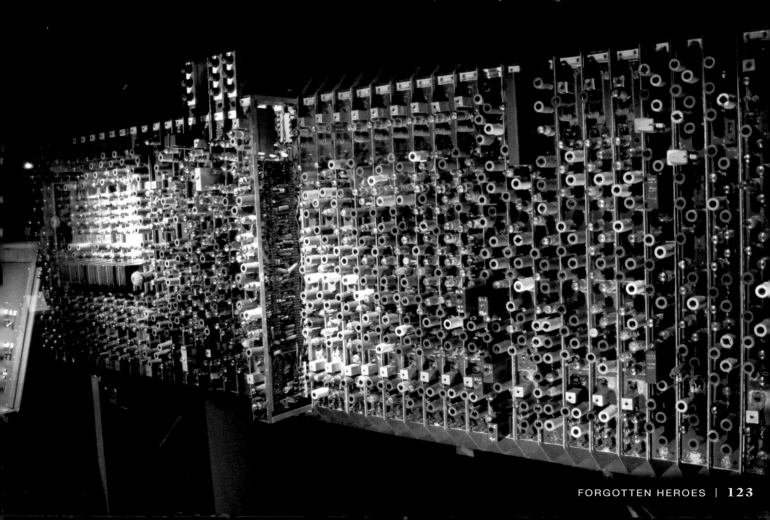

▼ The work of Ada Lovelace and other pioneers led to the creation of the first computers, such as this giant computer made by Alan Turing in the 1950s.

**A** | **Understanding the Gist.** Look back at your answer for exercise **E** on page 121. Was your prediction correct?

**B** | **Completing a Summary.** Complete the short biography about Ada Lovelace with information from the reading on pages 122–123.

Ada Lovelace lived during the _____ century. Her mother was a _____, and her father was the famous poet _____. When Lovelace was _____ years old, she met a professor named _____. He was building a calculating _____. Lovelace enjoyed math, and she was interested in his device. In 1843, Lovelace _____ a report about the machine and added her own ideas and notes. Her notes included an _____, which is a particular type of calculation. Modern mathematicians consider this calculation to be the first-ever _____. People who want the world to remember Lovelace created a day to celebrate her. Ada Lovelace Day is on _____ every year.

**C** | **Critical Thinking: Analyzing an Argument.** With a partner, complete the chart below about the reading on pages 122–123.

| | |
|---|---|
| What is the writer's opinion of Ada Lovelace? | |
| Who does the writer compare Ada Lovelace to? How are the people similar? | |
| What achievements does the writer describe? | |
| How is Ada Lovelace important today? | |

**D** | **Critical Thinking: Synthesizing.** Discuss the questions with a partner.

1. What are three things that al-Jazari and Ada Lovelace have in common?

2. Why do you think they are not as well known as Leonardo da Vinci and Steve Jobs?

**GOAL:** In this lesson, you are going to draft and edit sentences on the following topic:
***Explain why we should have a day to celebrate a particular inventor.***

A | Read the information below.

## Language for Writing: Simple Past

Use the simple past to talk about completed actions in the past:

Ada Lovelace **lived** in London, England.

Add *-ed* to the base form of a regular verb to form the simple past.

Add *-d* if the verb already ends in *-e*:

invent—invent**ed**          live—live**d**          translate—translate**d**

Make spelling changes for some verbs.
For verbs that end in consonant + *-y*, drop the *-y* and add *-ied*:

try—tr**ied**          study—stud**ied**          carry—carr**ied**

For most verbs that end in consonant + vowel + consonant, double the final consonant
and add *-ed.*

stop—stop**ped**          excel—excel**led**          rob—rob**bed**

Some verbs have irregular past forms:

| | | | |
|---|---|---|---|
| become—became | build—built | come—came | eat—ate |
| find—found | go—went | grow—grew | have—had |
| make—made | meet—met | put—put | say—said |

For negative statements, use *did not (didn't)* + the base form of a verb:
She **didn't invent** the analytical engine.

Now write the simple past form of each verb.

| Base Form | Simple Past Form | | Base Form | Simple Past Form |
|---|---|---|---|---|
| create | | | begin | |
| try | | | invent | |
| say | | | build | |
| have | | | grow up | |
| excel | | | go | |
| design | | | discover | |
| save | | | develop | |

**B** | Complete each sentence with the simple past form of the verb in parentheses.

1. Hungarian László Bíró _____ (*invent*) the first ballpoint pen in the early 1900s. Bíró's brother _____ (*help*) him with the invention. Bíró and his brother were born in Hungary, but they _____ (*go*) to Argentina in 1943. Bíró _____ (*die*) in 1985.

2. American secretary Bette Nesmith Graham _____ (*create*) liquid paper, also known as Wite-Out™. Nesmith Graham _____ (*come up with*) the idea when she was painting some windows. Nesmith Graham _____ (*put*) some paint in a bottle and brought it to the office. She _____ (*use*) the paint to cover up typing mistakes.

3. Archaeologists _____ (*find*) the world's first bars of soap in Babylon, which is in modern-day Iraq. Babylonians _____ (*mix*) animal fat with wood ashes and water to make the soap.

**C** | Write sentences (1–8) about yourself and people you know. Use the simple past tense of the verbs in parentheses.

1. I _____ (*go*).

2. I _____ (*not go*).

3. My teacher _____ (*say*).

4. My teacher _____ (*not say*).

5. My friends _____ (*come*).

6. They _____ (*not come*).

7. My friends and I _____ (*have*).

8. We _____ (*not have*).

**D** | Read the information below. Then complete each sentence (1–8) with the correct simple past form of *be*.

### Language for Writing: Simple Past of *be*

Use the simple past of *be* to describe people, things, and situations in the past. The verb *be* is usually followed by a noun, an adjective, or a prepositional phrase:

*Ada Lovelace **was** a mathematician.*

*She **was** talented.*

*Lovelace and Babbage **were** in London when they met.*

The past forms of *be* are *was/was not* and *were/were not*. You can use contractions for the negative forms: *wasn't* and *weren't*. We usually use contractions when we speak. We do not often use contractions in academic writing.

*Ada Lovelace **was not** a university professor.*

*Ada Lovelace and Alan Turing **were not** alive at the same time.*

For further explanation and examples of the simple past of *be*, see page 156.

1. Ada Lovelace _____ a mathematician.

2. She and Charles Babbage _____ friends.

3. Babbage _____ a professor.

4. Lovelace's parents _____ both successful people.

5. Her mother _____ an engineer.

6. Her father _____ the famous poet Lord Byron.

7. Al-Jazari _____ an engineer.

8. Al-Jazari and Ada Lovelace _____ doctors.

**E** | Write true sentences (1–4) about famous people in the past. Use the past tense of *be*. Write two affirmative sentences and two negative sentences.

1. _____.

2. _____.

3. _____.

4. _____.

**A** | **Brainstorming.** With a partner, write the names of two inventors and list their achievements. Write notes, not complete sentences. (Research online to find more information if necessary.)

| 1. _____ | 2. _____ |
| --- | --- |
| | |

**B** | **Planning.** Imagine your school will have a day to celebrate an inventor. Who should you celebrate? Circle one person above in your chart.

**C** | **Draft 1.** Use your ideas to write six sentences about the inventor. Use the simple past.

| Main idea | I think we should celebrate _____. |
| --- | --- |
| When and where did this person live? | _____ lived _____. |
| Main reason to celebrate this person | The main reason we should celebrate _____ is _____ _____. |
| A second reason | Another reason is _____ _____. |
| A third reason | Also, _____ _____. |
| What should people do on this day? | On this day, people should _____ _____. |

**D** | **Editing Checklist.** Use the checklist to find errors in your first draft.

| Editing Checklist | Yes | No |
| --- | --- | --- |
| 1. Are all the words spelled correctly? | | |
| 2. Is the first word of every sentence capitalized? | | |
| 3. Does every sentence end with the correct punctuation? | | |
| 4. Do your subjects and verbs agree? | | |
| 5. Did you use the simple past tense correctly? | | |

**E** | **Draft 2.** Use your Editing Checklist to write a second draft of your sentences. Make any other necessary changes.

# Alien Worlds

ACADEMIC PATHWAYS
Lesson A:  Taking Notes
            Inferring reasons and motivations
Lesson B:  Reading an article about new technology
Lesson C:  Writing sentences to express your opinion

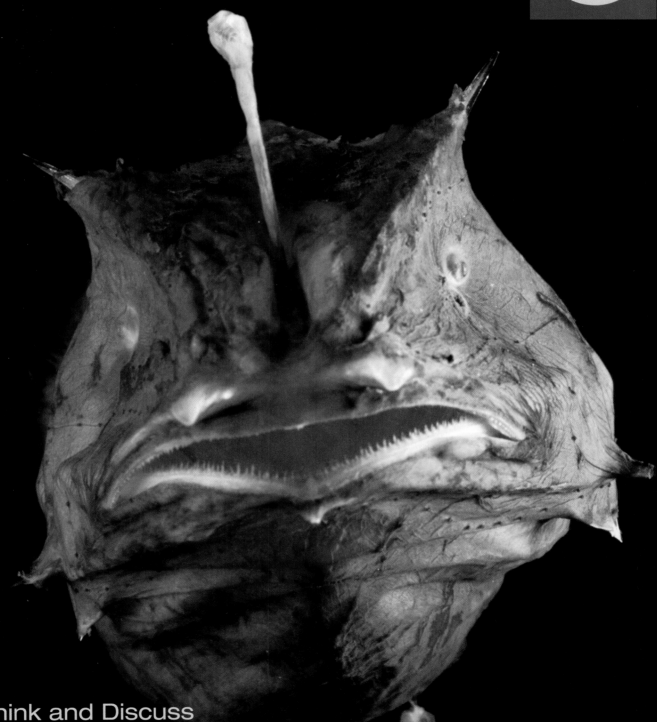

## Think and Discuss

1. What do you think is more interesting—
the ocean or space? Why?

2. Would you ever want to explore the ocean
or space? Why, or why not?

▲ The anglerfish is a predator
that lives near the bottom of
the ocean.

129

**A.** Look at the information on these two pages and answer the questions.

1. What do astronomers do?

2. What is the Milky Way? What do we know about it?

3. In which part of the Milky Way do we live?

**B.** Answer the questions about yourself.

1. Do you think there is life on other planets? Why, or why not?

2. In your opinion, what is the most surprising information on these two pages?

# Our Home in Space

The Milky Way Galaxy—our home— has hundreds of billions of stars. Our solar system—including the sun, Earth, Mars, Venus, and other planets—is in a part of the galaxy called the Orion Arm. The solar system may seem big to us, but it is really a small part of our galaxy. Light from one end of the galaxy would take 100,000 years to travel to the other side. However, the Milky Way is small compared to the universe. Astronomers—scientists who study space—think there are billions of galaxies beyond our Milky Way.

0°

30°

60°

90°

120°

150

10

SCUTUM

SAGITTA

PERSEUS ARM

O U T E

20,000

30,000

40,000

50,000 light-years

Direction of rotation

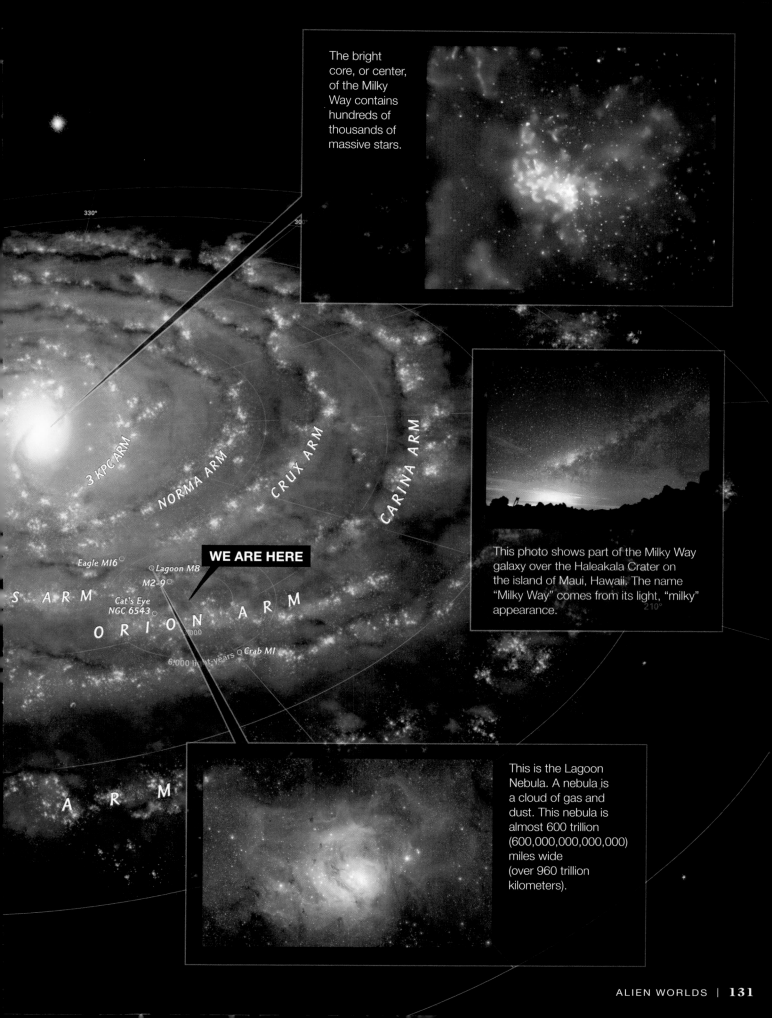

The bright core, or center, of the Milky Way contains hundreds of thousands of massive stars.

This photo shows part of the Milky Way galaxy over the Haleakala Crater on the island of Maui, Hawaii. The name "Milky Way" comes from its light, "milky" appearance.

This is the Lagoon Nebula. A nebula is a cloud of gas and dust. This nebula is almost 600 trillion (600,000,000,000,000) miles wide (over 960 trillion kilometers).

330°

300°

210°

3 KPC ARM

NORMA ARM

CRUX ARM

CARINA ARM

Eagle M16

Lagoon M8

M2-9

Cat's Eye
NGC 6543

WE ARE HERE

S   A R M

O R I O N   A R M

6,000 light-years

Crab M1

A R M

**A** | **Building Vocabulary.** Match the sentence parts (1–5 and a–e) to make definitions. Use a dictionary to help you.

**Word Partners**

Use **faraway** with nouns: faraway **planet**, faraway **galaxy**, faraway **land**.

1. _____ Use **faraway** to describe
2. _____ Use **certain** to refer to
3. _____ The **distance** between two places is
4. _____ The **temperature** of something is
5. _____ **Forms** of something are

a. particular or specific things.
b. types or kinds of it.
c. the amount of space between them.
d. something that is a long way from you.
e. how hot or cold it is.

**B** | **Building Vocabulary.** Complete each sentence (1–5) with the correct word from the box.

| bright | impossible | join | reach | size |

1. Astronauts went to the moon in the 1960s. Someday, they might _____ Mars.

2. What is the _____ of the Earth? It is about 25,000 miles (40,000 kilometers) across.

3. Some people think we can travel to Mars one day. Other people think that is _____.

4. When the sun is very _____ and it shines in your eyes, it can be difficult to see.

5. Are you interested in space exploration? If you are, you can _____ a club and study space with other people.

**C** | **Using Vocabulary.** Answer the questions. Share your ideas with a partner.

1. Which **faraway** country do you want to visit?

2. In your city, what is the average **temperature** in the winter? What is the average temperature in the summer?

3. What things are **impossible** now, but may be possible in the future?

**Word Link**

**im** = not:
**im**possible, **im**mature, **im**patient, **im**polite, **im**perfect

**D** | **Predicting.** Look at the title and images on pages 133–134. What do you think the reading is about?

a. the history of space exploration

b. the cost of space technology

c. the search for planets like Earth

# OTHER WORLDS

track **2-10**

**A**     **LOOK UP AT THE SKY** on a dark, moonless night. What do you see? There are many thousands of stars. But are there other planets like Earth?

**B**     New technology is helping astronomers discover hundreds of **faraway** planets. So far, we know of more than 500 "exoplanets." These are planets that move around stars other than the sun. Some exoplanets may be similar to our own.

**C**     An Earthlike exoplanet must have **certain** characteristics. It needs to be the right **distance** from its star. Then it will be the right **temperature** for living things—not too cold and not too hot. A planet at the right distance might also have water. Where there is water, there might be **forms** of life.

**D**     In October 2012, scientists were excited to find a new exoplanet. The planet moves around Alpha Centauri, the nearest star system[1] to us. The planet is similar in **size** to Earth. But there is a problem: The temperature there is about 1,500 degrees Celsius. Life on Alpha Centauri's planet is **impossible**. But life forms might exist on planets not yet discovered.

[1] A **star system** is a group of planets and other objects in space that orbit, or travel around, a star.

## Planet Hunters

E    Now astronomers are not the only people searching for exoplanets. Anyone can **join** the search. For example, you can join a crowdsourcing project called Zooniverse. Volunteers study images from the Kepler space telescope.[2] They look for patterns in the brightness of stars. As a planet passes in front of a star, the star becomes less **bright**. So a star with changing brightness might have its own planet.

## Moving to Another World?

▲ In the future, a starship like this might carry thousands of people to a new home planet.

F    If we do find an Earthlike planet, it might be possible for humans to live there. But will we ever **reach** it? The biggest problem is distance. The closest star system, Alpha Centauri, is 4.3 light-years[3] from Earth. Traveling there with today's technology would take thousands of years.

G    In the future, however, traveling to another world might be possible. Scientist Andreas Tziolas thinks we might one day use a technology called nuclear fusion. A fusion-powered starship could reach the nearest star in a few decades. "I believe we can achieve some form of interstellar[4] exploration within a hundred years," he says.

---

[2] A **telescope** is an instrument that makes distant things look bigger and nearer when you look through it.

[3] A **light-year** is the distance that light travels in one year. It equals about 5.88 trillion (5,880,000,000,000) miles or 9.46 trillion (9,460,000,000,000) kilometers.

[4] If something is **interstellar**, it occurs between two or more stars.

**A** | **Understanding the Gist.** Look back at your answer for exercise **D** on page 132. Was your prediction correct?

**B** | **Identifying Key Details.** What are three characteristics of an Earthlike planet? Complete the notes with details from the reading on pages 133–134.

Characteristics of an Earthlike planet:

1. at right _____ from its star

2. at right _____—not too cold or hot for living things

3. has _____—important for all life forms

**C** | **Understanding Problems and Solutions.** Complete the chart with information from pages 133–134.

| Problems | Solutions |
|---|---|
| **1. Analyzing data**<br><br>The Kepler space telescope collects data. Scientists need help to analyze the data. | _____Volunteers_____ can join a _____ project called Zooniverse. |
| **2. Reaching an exoplanet**<br><br>The biggest challenge is _____.<br><br>Alpha Centauri is the closest _____. It is _____ away from us. With today's technology, it would take _____ to reach it. | In the future, we might use _____ technology. It will help us reach Alpha Centauri in _____.<br><br>According to Andreas Tziolas, we may be able to explore other stars _____ from now. |

 **D** | **Critical Thinking: Inferring Reasons.** Discuss these questions with a partner.

1. What might we learn from studying exoplanets?
2. Why do you think some people are looking for ways to reach an exoplanet?

**Reading Skill:** *Taking Notes*

Taking notes as you read can help you remember key information in a passage. It can help you understand how a passage is organized. It will also help you remember key ideas for a writing task or test.

As you read, note key nouns such as names, places, and times. Include details about each one. Also, note how ideas and information relate to each other. For example, note any causes and effects, problems and solutions, steps in a process, or events in a story.

It can be helpful to note information using an outline or a graphic organizer. Here is one example:

Outline
Main Idea
    Detail
    Detail
Main Idea
    Detail
    Detail

Remember not to use complete sentences. Also, use symbols and abbreviations in your notes. Here are some common examples:

| | | | |
|---|---|---|---|
| **& or +** (and) | **=** (is the same as; means) | **~** (around; about) | **b/c** (because) |
| **para** (paragraph) | **p. / pp.** (page / pages) | **info** (information) | **incl** (including) |
| **e.g.** (for example) | **> / <** (more than / less than) | **ppl** (people) | **chg** (change) |

**A** | **Taking Notes in an Outline.** Complete the outline using information from pages 133–134.

p. 133 Para B
- astronomers use new _____ to find exoplanets
- so far, found > _____
- some may be like _____

p. 134 Para E
- astronomers & _____ are searching
- ppl study _____ from space telescope
- look for _____ in star brightness
- less bright = _____ passing in front of star?

**B** | **Applying.** Now create your own outline for Paragraph **D** on page 133.

# Mapping the Labyrinth

◄ These divers are part of an international team that explored and mapped part of the Wakulla Springs underwater cave system in Florida, USA.

## Before Viewing

**A | Using a Dictionary.** Here are some words you will hear in the video. Complete each definition with the correct word. Use your dictionary to help you.

> current        labyrinth        three-dimensional

1. If something is _____, it is not flat and it has a shape.

2. If there is a _____ in water, the water moves in one direction.

3. A _____ is an area with many tunnels or paths. It's easy to get lost in one.

**B | Thinking Ahead.** Look at the photo above and read the caption. Why do you think cave diving might be dangerous? What might people learn from cave diving? Discuss your ideas with a partner.

## While Viewing

Read the questions (1–3). Think about the answers as you watch the video.

1. What happens to Boyd Matson, the narrator, as he moves through the caves?

2. What technology do they use to map the caves?

3. How can the team's project help people who can't go cave diving?

## After Viewing

**A |** Discuss the answers to the questions (1–3) above with a partner.

**B | Synthesizing.** In what ways are the divers in the video similar to people who want to travel into space?

**A** | **Building Vocabulary.** Read the sentences below. Write each word in **bold** next to its definition (1–5).

Most of space is a **mystery** to us. We don't know much about it.

A layer of gray dust **covers** the moon. The dust is everywhere, and it caused problems for astronauts when they landed on the moon.

Over 96 **percent** of Earth's water is in the oceans.

The moon's **surface** is dry and has a lot of holes in it.

You have to use a special **vehicle** to explore deep parts of the ocean.

1. _____: something that you cannot explain or understand

2. _____: %; part of 100

3. _____: a machine that transports people or things from one place to another

4. _____: forms a layer over the top of something

5. _____: the outside of something

**B** | **Building Vocabulary.** Read the definitions below. Then complete each sentence (1–5) with the correct word.

**Word Partners**

Use **variety** with *of* and a noun:
variety **of activities**,
variety **of colors**,
variety **of foods**,
variety **of products**,
variety **of styles**,
variety **of sizes**.

Something that is **beneath** another thing is under it.

A **variety** of something is a number of different kinds or examples of it.

An **illness** is a particular disease, or a period of being sick.

If you **complete** a task or a journey, you finish it.

The **beginning** of something is the first part of it.

1. There is a _____ of reasons that people decide to study space. For example, some want to find life on other planets. Others want to know how the universe started.

2. In 1840, the British explorer Sir James Clark Ross used a tool to get samples from the ocean floor. Some experts think this was the _____ of deep-sea exploration.

3. If you have an _____ like a cold or the flu, you should not go swimming in the ocean.

4. There is a layer of hot melted rock _____ the surface of the Earth.

5. In 22 years, the space shuttle *Columbia* was able to _____ 27 flights into space.

**C | Using Vocabulary.** Answer the questions (1–4) in complete sentences. Then share your sentences with a partner.

1. There are some places and objects on Earth that are **mysteries**—we are not exactly sure how or why people created them. Describe one of Earth's mysteries.

   _____

   _____

2. Is there a **variety** of restaurants in your town or city? What are some examples?

   _____

   _____

3. What do you do when a good friend or family member has an **illness** like a cold or the flu?

   _____

   _____

4. What is one task you **completed** recently? How did you feel when you completed it?

   _____

   _____

**D | Expanding Vocabulary.** Match each word (1–10) to its synonym (a–j). Use a dictionary if you don't know the meaning of a word.

| | | |
|---|---|---|
| _j_ 1. complete | a. top part | |
| ___ 2. surface | b. sickness | |
| ___ 3. certain | c. get to | |
| ___ 4. beneath | d. hard | |
| ___ 5. illness | e. types | |
| ___ 6. difficult | f. under | |
| ___ 7. data | g. start | |
| ___ 8. beginning | h. specific | |
| ___ 9. reach | i. information | |
| ___ 10. forms | j. finish | |

> **Word Usage**
>
> **Synonyms** are words that have the same or similar meanings such as *complete* and *finish*. Use a thesaurus to find synonyms for new words you learn. This way you can learn several new words at one time.

**E | Predicting.** Look at the title, subheads, and photos of the reading on pages 140–141. What do you think the passage is mainly about?

a. protecting deep-sea animals

b. exploring deep parts of the ocean

c. how underwater mountains form

# Hidden Depths

track 2-11

**A** OCEANS HAVE ALWAYS seemed mysterious. In the past, people believed that giant serpents[1] and dragons lived in the sea. Other people imagined mermaids[2] and underwater cities.

**B** Today, much of the world's oceans are still a **mystery**. "The oceans **cover** 71 **percent** of our planet," says oceanography professor Dr. Robert Ballard. "Yet only five percent of it has been explored." In fact, we know more about the **surface** of Mars than about some parts of the world's oceans.

## Mountains in the Sea

**C** New technology, however, is helping scientists explore these hidden worlds. For example, scientists are using an underwater **vehicle** called DeepSee to explore seamounts. These are underwater mountains **beneath** the ocean's surface.

**D** Scientists used DeepSee to study Las Gemelas, an area of seamounts near Costa Rica. A huge **variety** of species lives on and around Las Gemelas. One type of fish—the orange roughy—can live for more than 100 years. Scientists are also finding species never seen before. Some may have chemicals that can help people fight **illnesses**, such as cancer.

## Down in the Depths

**E** The deepest place on Earth is the Mariana Trench in the Pacific Ocean. The ocean floor there is about 36,000 feet (11,000 meters) deep. In 2012, filmmaker and explorer James Cameron reached the Mariana Trench in a vehicle called Deep Sea Challenger. He was the first person to **complete** the journey alone. Cameron took photos and video on the ocean floor. He also collected underwater samples.[3]

**F** Vehicles such as Deep Sea Challenger are helping us discover new animals and plants. Some of these have existed for millions of years. These discoveries could help us better understand how life began. Deep-sea exploration also helps us in other ways. For example, we are learning how underwater earthquakes cause tsunamis. As Cameron says, "This is the **beginning** of opening up [a] new frontier."[4]

[1] A **serpent** is a snake, usually a very large one.
[2] In stories, a **mermaid** is a woman who has a fish's tail and lives in the ocean.
[3] **Samples** are small amounts of something that show you what the rest of it is like.
[4] A **frontier** is a place that people are just starting to live in or explore.

Frogfish

Anglerfish

Comb jelly

Sea stars

Humboldt squid

Sea walnut

Squid embryo

Hatchet fish

▲ Underwater vehicles such as DeepSee (above) are shining a light on mysterious deep-sea creatures, such as the ones shown here.

**A** | **Understanding the Gist.** Look back at your answer for exercise **E** on page 139. Was your prediction correct?

**B** | **Identifying Key Details.** Use the outline to take notes on the reading on pages 140–141.

(Paras A and B) Oceans = mystery

    cover _____ of Earth

    expl'd _____

    we know more about _____

(Paras C and D) New tech. ⟶ explore more

    vehicle called _____

    went to _____ near _____

(Paras E and F) Deepest place in ocean = _____

    2012: _____ explored alone

    he took _____ and collected _____

    deep-sea vehicles help us understand how _____

    also learn about how _____ cause _____

**C** | **Critical Thinking: Meaning from Context.** The words below are synonyms for words in the reading on pages 140–141. Scan the reading to find the correct synonyms.

1. (Paragraph A) dreamed _____

2. (Paragraph C) unseen _____

3. (Paragraph F) findings _____

4. (Paragraph F) start _____

**D** | **Critical Thinking: Analyzing an Argument.** Complete the chart below with information from the reading passage.

| | | |
|---|---|---|
| What do ocean scientists and explorers do? | | |
| Why is their work useful? (What are some possible benefits?) | | |

**E** | **Synthesizing.** Look back at your answer to question 1 on page 129. Has your opinion changed? Complete the sentence and list two reasons. Share your ideas in a small group.

I think _____ exploration is more interesting.

Reason 1: _____

Reason 2: _____

> **GOAL:** In this lesson, you are going to draft and edit sentences on the following topic:
> ***Express your opinion about space and ocean exploration.***

**A** | Read the information below.

## Language for Writing: Introducing Your Opinion

You can use these expressions to introduce an opinion, or what you think about something:

> ***I think*** *we can reach Mars someday.*
>
> ***I don't think*** *we can reach Mars someday.*
>
> ***I believe*** *there are other forms of life in the universe.*
>
> ***I don't believe*** *there are other forms of life in the universe.*

You can also use the expression *in my opinion*. To form a negative statement with this expression, use a negative verb form in the main part of the sentence. Remember to use a comma after *in my opinion*.

> ***In my opinion****, people will live on Mars someday.*
>
> ***In my opinion****, people will not live on Mars someday.*

Now complete the sentences (1–6) to make statements about your opinions.
Use the correct forms of the words in parentheses in the last two sentences (5–6).

### think / don't think

1. I _____ humans will live in space 50 years from now.

2. I _____ scientists will discover life on Mars.

### believe / don't believe

3. I _____ it's important to spend a lot of money on space exploration.

4. I _____ governments should spend more money on exploration than on education.

### In my opinion, / In my opinion, . . . not

5. _____, the Earth (*be*) _____ the only planet in the universe with life on it.

6. _____, astronomers (*have*) _____ a more interesting job than ocean explorers do.

**B** | Write your opinion about each of the ideas below (1–3). In each sentence, use a different phrase to introduce your opinion.

**Example:** Space exploration can help us learn about our own planet.

*I believe space exploration can help us learn about our own planet.*

1. Studying the ocean can teach us how life began.

_____

2. Life forms from other planets are looking for us.

_____

3. People will live on an exoplanet 100 years from now.

_____

**C** | Read the information below.

**Language for Writing:** Using *Should*

The word *should* is a modal. We use it to give advice or talk about the right thing to do. We use a base form of a verb with *should*. To make a negative statement, use *not* after *should*:

*You **should read** this article about deep-sea exploration.*
*People **should join** crowdsourcing projects because they're fun.*
*Divers **should not damage** coral reefs because sea animals live in them.*

To form a question, use *should* + a subject + the base form of a verb:

***Should we join** this crowdsourcing project?*

You can introduce an opinion with *should* by using one of the expressions on page 143:

***I think** people **should** join crowdsourcing projects because they're fun.*
***I don't think** people **should** swim near coral reefs because they might damage them.*

Now unscramble the words and phrases to make sentences (1–4).

1. not / leave now / we / so we're / late / should / .

_____

2. I / take / semester / astronomy / should / this / ?

_____

3. should / class / take / you / an oceanography / .

_____

4. should / she / not / the ocean during / the winter / go diving in / .

_____

**D** | Think of a foreign country you have visited or would like to visit. What should people do or not do when they visit that country? Complete each sentence (1–6) with *should* or *should not*.

1. You _____ try to learn the local language before you visit.

2. You _____ travel alone.

3. You _____ carry a lot of cash.

4. You _____ stay in large hotels in the big cities.

5. You _____ give tips (money) to restaurant and hotel workers.

6. (your own idea) _____

**E** | Complete the chart with things people *should* and *should not* do when they are learning a new language.

| When people are learning a new language, | |
|---|---|
| ***they should . . .*** | ***they should not . . .*** |
| study every day | |

Now use the information above to write three affirmative sentences (using *should*) and one negative sentence (using *should not*). Use a different opinion expression in each sentence.

**Example:** I think language learners should study every day.

1. _____

2. _____

3. _____

4. _____

**A** | **Brainstorming.** With a partner, look for information in this unit to complete the chart. Add more ideas of your own.

| Astronomers study space because . . . | Ocean scientists study the sea because . . . |
| --- | --- |
| | |

**B** | **Planning.** Look at your ideas in exercise **A**. Which do you think is more important—space exploration or ocean exploration?

**C** | **Draft 1.** Use your ideas to answer this question: *What should governments spend more money on—space exploration or ocean exploration?* Use opinion expressions and *should*.

| **Main idea** | _____ **governments** _____ **spend more money on** _____ **exploration.** |
| --- | --- |
| Reason 1 | With _____ exploration, we can learn more about _____. |
| Reason 2 | Also, _____ _____. |
| Reason 3 | In addition, _____. |
| Reason 4 | Finally, governments _____ because _____. |

**D** | **Editing Checklist.** Use the checklist to find errors in your first draft.

| **Editing Checklist** | **Yes** | **No** |
| --- | --- | --- |
| 1. Are all the words spelled correctly? | | |
| 2. Is the first word of every sentence capitalized? | | |
| 3. Does every sentence end with the correct punctuation? | | |
| 4. Do your subjects and verbs agree? | | |
| 5. Did you use expressions to introduce your opinion correctly? | | |
| 6. Did you use *should* correctly? | | |

**E** | **Draft 2.** Use your Editing Checklist to write a second draft of your sentences. Make any other necessary changes.

## UNIT 1

# 7 Billion

This video has on-screen text only.

## UNIT 2

# Killer Crocs

**Narrator:** Nile crocodiles are the most aggressive crocs on the planet. In the area of Lake Victoria in Uganda, they've been attacking and killing humans. Why are these crocs so aggressive? People in the nearby villages are killing or driving away the animals that the crocs eat. Without their natural food sources, the crocs are now attacking people. Sometimes they even pull them out of their fishing boats. And now, this behavior is increasing.

To save both the people and crocodiles, the Ugandan government asked National Geographic's Dr. Brady Barr for help.

**Dr. Brady Barr:** I've offered to help catch the animals and relocate them to a place where they can do no harm. And at the same time, I'll train local wildlife rangers to capture crocodiles so that they can respond to future attacks.

**Narrator:** Brady's first two students are rangers Robert Mbagaya and Peter Ogwang. Both men have over ten years, experience with dangerous animals. But they don't have any experience with crocodiles. First, Brady shows the men how to catch crocodiles.

**Dr. Barr:** Don't ever wrap the rope around your hand, because if you do, the crocodile can pull you into the water. Or if it's a big crocodile, it can rip your hand off. In the past, if a crocodile attacked a person, the rangers would have to shoot and kill it.

**Narrator:** Brady explains to them that now they can catch the animal alive, tie it up, and take it to a safer place. After Brady teaches the rangers some techniques, it's time to catch a croc.

Robert sees the first croc under a tree.

**Dr. Barr:** Peter, come in and catch it. Just come in and get it. Come in and get it.

**Narrator:** Peter carefully comes near the croc. Brady is close by.

**Dr. Barr:** Don't pull, or you won't get it. Let me make his head come my direction. Just keep it right there. OK there you go. Now fix your snare. Now, take your time. Get it on the upper jaw. Put it on the upper jaw. Just the upper jaw. Come closer, go closer. He needs to see your body, Peter. Now, take your time. Come on, take your time. Tighten it; pull back, tight! All right, we got it. Pull him out! You got it?

**Ranger:** Yeah, got it.

**Dr. Barr:** Hurry, Robert! Go around there and help him pull the animal towards Graham. Hurry, Robert. Pull him! Keep pulling! OK that's good, that's good. OK. Pull a little more, a little more. Hang on.

**Narrator:** Now Robert's got to close the jaws.

**Dr. Barr:** Now, pull, pull! Tight! Quick! Come here! Charles, hold the rope. Jump on its neck. Just jump on its neck. Good job! All right, Robert, go onto the back. Pull the legs up. Hurry, hurry, hurry, before it rolls. Let it roll! Get on there, Peter! You gotta sit on it. OK. Sit down right there. Whew, man! Put 'er there. You caught your first crocodile all by yourself.

**Narrator:** Uganda now has two rangers who are ready to catch the killer crocs of Lake Victoria.

**Dr. Barr:** I'm going to leave the snare pole and all the equipment with you.

**Ranger:** Thank you.

**Dr. Barr:** You're very welcome.

**Ranger:** What I want to do for my country is rescue these crocodiles. That way, our local people will be safe and their lives will be protected.

**Narrator:** Months later, Peter helps to catch and move one of the killer crocs. This way, he is creating a safer environment for both people and crocodiles.

## UNIT 3

# Crossing America

**Narrator:** Today, most American citizens probably don't think much about how their country's transportation system began. It's now very easy to get from place to place. A New York businessman can easily get to an important meeting in Los Angeles. A ride to the airport, a direct flight, and after a few short hours, you can be on the west coast of America.

Millions of Americans take trips like this every year. But traveling across North America wasn't always so easy. It took 200 years of innovations, creativity, and hard work to get where we are today.

This transportation revolution actually began in the 1800s with a lot of hot air. Engineer Robert Fulton used a steam engine to power his boat, up the Hudson River – a journey of around 150 miles. Fulton's trip was a big success. And in a few years, there were steamboats on many of America's rivers.

There were innovations on land too. In 1830, inventor Peter Cooper built a small, steam-powered train called "Tom Thumb". Train travel became popular, and thousands of miles of new railroad tracks were built. The tracks connected almost every major city in the eastern United States. But Americans wanted to do more and go even further.

The next goal was to connect the east coast to the west. In 1869, after six years of hard work, the nation's first transcontinental railroad was completed. Before, a trip from New York to California could take many months. Now, people could travel coast to coast in just a few days.

The transcontinental railroad had a huge impact on the west. People built new towns near the railroad tracks, and cities grew quickly. Industry and business boomed. And for the first time, Americans began commuting to work.

New ways of traveling appeared on the ground and underground. In San Francisco and other cities, people began using streetcars, or cable cars, to get around. By 1904, New York City opened its first subway line. Today it's one of the largest in the world.

At the same time, Americans were also exploring air travel. The world's first successful flight was in 1903 by American brothers Orville and Wilbur Wright.

Eleven years later, the country's first airline company started doing business. Since that day, aircraft have become bigger, faster, and safer. Now, America has about 70 commercial airlines. It's the largest and busiest air transportation system in the world, with more than 35,000 flights leaving from American airports every day.

Two hundred years ago, long distance travel was difficult and took days or weeks. Now, you can cross from the east to the west coast of America in just a few hours. These innovations in travel have brought us a very long way.

## UNIT 4
# Arctic Flyer

**Narrator:** Gus McLeod is following his dream. And it will be a test of endurance and skill. Gus plans to break a record— by flying to the North Pole in a vintage, open cockpit biplane.

**Gus McLeod:** There's not a lot of challenges left for the common man. But I just like adventure. This is a good adventure.

**Narrator:** Gus knows flying his 1939 Stearman biplane to the North Pole won't be easy. Especially in an open cockpit. Gus knows he'll face some risks, but he's convinced he can do it.

**McLeod:** I think I can pull this off because I'm persistent, I'm determined, and I think I have the skills to do it.

**Narrator:** The route he'll take is more than 3,000 miles long. He will take off from Maryland, fly all the way to the Canadian Arctic, and land at the North Pole.

Sunday, April 2nd: A crowd gathers to cheer Gus as he takes off.

**McLeod:** Thank you for coming out again and I'll see you when I get back.

**Narrator:** But after take off, a loose wheel cover forces Gus to make an emergency landing. After three days of bad weather, Gus finally takes off again. He flies over 500 miles, to Ontario, Canada.

There's heavy snow in Ontario. It's going to be very chilly for Gus. Just after he takes off, he flies into a snowstorm.

**McLeod:** This is amazing. I'm encountering conditions I shouldn't be encountering for another 500 miles.

**Narrator:** Gus flies 800 miles in freezing temperatures.

**McLeod:** The only thing I can feel is numb. My feet hurt, my hands hurt, my whole body aches. I can't even shiver, it's so cold.

**Narrator:** But it's still more than 2,000 miles to the North Pole and it's going to get a lot colder now.

**McLeod:** This has been a tough flight. We haven't even gotten to the Arctic yet. I've got to re-think this.

**Narrator:** But Gus decides to continue.

**McLeod:** It's now or never. I've got to go.

**Narrator:** Day nine: It's minus 23 degrees and the wind makes it feel even colder. Gus dresses in six layers, including a specially made Arctic suit. For mile after mile, all he sees is ice and snow. Gus flies over 1,000 miles to the Arctic Circle. This far north, the sun is up for nearly 24 hours. He has just a little farther to go. And Gus is ready to take off again.

Gus is going to stop for fuel on the ice pack. From there, it's just 280 more miles to the Pole.

After nearly three hours of flying, Gus is close to the fuel, but he will have to land on the ice without skis.

Now, the final part of the trip. He's there. He flies a few times around the pole.

**Radio Air Traffic Control:** Gus, congratulations on flying to the North Pole.

**Narrator:** But there's no time to celebrate. Now, he's got to fly back. And on the way the plane engine starts stalling . . . it stops three times and Gus barely makes it to Eureka.

Gus decides he can't fly it the rest of the way. He feels good about his achievement, but a little sad, too.

**McLeod:** I'm glad I did it. I haven't paid the full cost of what this trip has been. I haven't paid the full cost physically. And I haven't paid the full cost emotionally.

**Narrator:** But Gus broke a record, and it was an extraordinary achievement.

## UNIT 5
# Citizen Scientists

**Dr. Fredrik Hiebert:** The Burkhan Kaldun, it's not just a mountain. It's a whole mountain range. It's more than 12,000 square kilometers. To begin to investigate that area, it would take more than 100 archaeologists all their lives just to begin to look.

**Dr. Albert Yu-Min Lin:** So we're asking the public to scan the entire area through the human computation network and tell us where to go so we can find any possible traces of Burkhan Kaldun.

**Narrator:** To find the tomb of Genghis Khan, Dr. Lin's team use what they call a "human computation network". The team shared 85,000 satellite images of the region on their website. Citizen scientists around the world scan the images and tag anything that looks unusual. Some of these might be ancient structures.

**Dr. Lin:** This is the data that just came in today, huh?

**Member of team:** Mm-hmm. These are the most recent tags that have been uploaded onto the data pads.

**Dr. Lin:** Hundreds of our citizen scientists tagged this unusual rectangle shape on the satellite map. Straight lines are usually a good indicator that something's man-made. The site is less than two miles from our camp. Could it be the tomb of Genghis Khan? We're going to go check it out.

We're going to scan every single one of the human computation sites that have been picked out on that mountain and try to figure out what people saw.

**Narrator:** Lin and his team get on horses and ride out to the site. There, they find something interesting.

**Dr. Lin:** We come upon this thing, this thing that was identified by the public, made of rocks sticking out of the earth. This is it.

**Dr. Hiebert:** It's clearly a tomb, but it's too old to be Genghis Khan's. It's Bronze Age, it's more than 3,000 years old.

**Dr. Lin:** Well you can see this is a very well structured rectangular shape, these rocks set up like a home, you know. And the opening there represents a door, and always the door is facing south, so south is directly that way. I mean if people hundreds of miles can guide us through satellite images to this ancient grave site, then I feel like we've got a chance to find the tomb of Genghis Khan.

## UNIT 6 — Wonders of Madidi

**Narrator:** Joel Sartore is a National Geographic photographer. Today, he is in Madidi National Park in Bolivia - one of the last great tropical rainforests left on earth. It's full of amazing wildlife - birds, reptiles, even man-eating pigs.

Madidi National Park is almost 19,000 square kilometers and the only way to see it is by boat or on foot. Rosa Maria Ruiz is a conservationist for the park and will be Joel's guide. She is working to prevent the Bolivian government from building a dam here. The dam could destroy a lot of the park. For the next three weeks, she and her team are showing Joel the animals of the jungle.

**Joel Sartore:** Well, it's been about two hours and the fog has finally lifted. They're really moving fast. This is tough. This isn't easy. Oh, man, right when I'm changing film.

**Narrator:** Many creatures come out during the night in the jungle. Joel sets up a bug light by hanging a big sheet behind an ultraviolet light. Bugs are attracted to the light, and then he'll be able to photograph them.

**Sartore:** I'm hoping that it draws more moths in than anything else, and beetles. But a lot of nights all you get are stinging ants and flying ants and wasps and nasty things. I'm just hoping to get the pretty stuff.

Look at these bugs.

**Narrator:** There are bugs which look like a tree, and ones which have wings like a leaf.

**Sartore:** That's one of the stinging ones. Golly.

**Narrator:** There are so many bugs flying around, he even swallows one by mistake.

**Sartore:** Look at the diversity in these insects. You know that this is just a wonderful place. Thousands and thousands of species and insects, just drawn into this one light, one night. That indicates that we've really got a treasure here as far as the amount of habitat that's intact.

I've been here for over a week now and I think it's time to get the macaws.

This is day two trying to get the macaws in flight.

This is my fourth day up here.

This is day six up here and I think they're mocking me.

Excellent today, finally a good day. Tons of birds in the air. This is great.

Madidi is one of the most incredible places I've ever been and I want to share it with the world. It's also one of the last untouched places on Earth, and if the Bolivian government really builds a dam here, a lot of it will disappear. I hope my pictures make a difference.

## UNIT 7 — The Golden Age

**Isabella:** Is that the Librarian?

**Danny:** I guess so.

**Luke:** How are the Dark Ages gonna have anything to do with us?

**Danny:** Erm . . . excuse me, sorry to bother you.

**Librarian:** What do you want?

**Danny:** We need to find out what impact the Dark Ages had on the modern world?

**Librarian:** Never was a period of history so poorly named.

**Librarian:** Don't touch. It's priceless . . . Follow me. I've got just the book for you.

**Isabella:** Where are we going?

**Danny:** Don't know.

**Luke:** Ask him?

**Danny:** Uh, excuse me . . . where are we going?

**Librarian:** From darkness into light, my young friend. From ocean onto land. There are things you should know. Oh yes, indeed.

**Librarian:** Now, take a look . . . if you dare.

**Danny:** What's going on?!

**Librarian:** Welcome to the Dark Ages . . . or as it should be known, The Golden Ages.

**Isabella:** Who are you?

**Al-Jazari:** I am Al-Jazari, engineer and ingenious inventor.

**Luke:** I thought you said this was the Dark Ages. It doesn't look very . . . dark.

**Al-Jazari:** Of course there are parts of the world that weren't dark at all, but in a civilization that stretched from Spain to China the golden rays of discovery and invention shone over everything.

**Luke:** What civilization?

**Al-Jazari:** The Muslim civilization, my young friend. Through scholars and scientists of various faiths some of the most important discoveries known to man were made at this time.

**Danny:** Like what?

**Al-Jazari:** Well, all sorts of things.

**Luke:** I've gotta get a picture of this.

**Ibn al Haytham:** I knew it was a good idea.

**Isabella:** Who are you?

**Al-Jazari:** Allow me to introduce Ibn al-Haytham, a great scientist whose ideas led to the invention of the camera.

**Danny:** You invented the camera?

**Ibn al-Haytham:** I laid the foundations for modern cameras by explaining how our eyes work. I found a way of projecting an image onto another surface through a small hole in a dark room – later called *camera obscura*.

**Al-Jazari:** Think of all the things that evolved from this discovery – cameras, cinema, all share the same principle.

**Danny:** Cool.

**Ibn Firnas:** LOOK OUT BELOW!!

**Kids:** Who's that?

**Al-Jazari:** That's my good friend, Abbas ibn Firnas, who gazed up to the heavens passionate in his belief that man could fly.

**Luke:** Whoa.

**Al-Jazari:** You know you all take your jetsetting holidays for granted so it only seems fair to remember Abbas ibn Firnas . . . Science at its brilliant best!

**Luke:** And all these things were developed during the Golden Ages?

**Al-Jazari:** That's just the tip of the iceberg. There were thousands of other inventions covering all areas of life and in the years that followed their influence spread across the whole of medieval Europe so you see, it wasn't so dark after all.

**Danny:** What about you?

**Al-Jazari:** Me?

**Isabella:** What did you invent?

**Al-Jazari:** Well I don't want to be big-headed but I made some groundbreaking advances in engineering. I suppose . . . my crowning glory was my amazing time-telling machine, my legendary Elephant Clock.

**Danny:** It's a clock?

**Al-Jazari:** Yes.

**Al-Jazari:** Dozens of components collected from different cultures around the world – Indian, Greek, Arabian, Egyptian, Chinese.

**Luke:** Wow, a United Nations clock.

**Isabella:** That is pretty cool.

**Danny:** Does it actually tell the time?

**Al-Jazari:** Well, yes, of course. If it wasn't for me thousands of people would be late for everything. Speaking of time we better get you back. And remember, spread the word, this was a Golden Age, and I have only shown you a tiny part of this wondrous time.

**Danny:** No, wait! Whoa!

# Mapping the Labyrinth

UNIT 8

**Narrator:** In Florida, there is a series of underwater caves and tunnels. It's an area called Wakulla Springs, which some say means "mysterious waters."

A group of divers are exploring these underwater labyrinths. The divers are Jill Heinerth and Mark Meadows. Experienced explorer, Dr. Bill Stone, leads the team.

**Dr Bill Stone:** This is raw exploration. That is what drives most of our underwater teams onward.

**Narrator:** Some people consider cave diving to be the most dangerous sport in the world. Since 1960, about 300 divers have died in the caves and tunnels around north Florida. It's very easy to get lost.

To understand the risks of cave diving, TV presenter Boyd Matson joins a dive to an underwater cave at Ginnie Springs in Florida. This simple dive shows Matson how dangerous cave diving can be. Minutes in, he makes a big mistake – a mistake that has killed other cave divers. As he tries to get through a narrow opening, he kicks up a lot of sand. He finally gets through. But when he turns around, he can't see. The tunnel he just swam through will take hours to clear. Luckily, he has a rope to lead him out of the cave. Without the rope, he wouldn't find his way out.

This diving project aims to create the world's first digital three-dimensional map of an underwater cave system. Mark and Jill will make the next mapping dive at Wakulla Springs. Matson is helping to prepare the bell that will bring the divers out of the water at the end of the exploration.

With everything ready, the team starts their dive. They will have to drive this mapping machine through the tunnels. The machine bounces sound waves off the walls to create a map of the tunnels.

A thousand feet into the tunnel, there is a very strong current. Mark and Jill are very experienced cave divers. But other expert divers have lost their lives in situations like this. The team moves deeper into the labyrinth. On the surface, the rest of the team waits. At last, they see the flash of a dive light.

Jill and Mark have reached the end of the tunnel safely. They get into the diving bell and are soon at the surface. The exploration is very successful. Bill's team achieved its goal - a three-dimensional map of Wakulla Springs.

**Dr Stone:** Exploration is a physical process of putting your foot in places where humans have never stepped before.

# Contents

▲ **Vulnerable:** A young female Diana monkey

# Tips for Reading and Note Taking

## Reading fluently

Why develop your reading speed?

Reading slowly, one word at a time, makes it difficult to understand the meaning of a text. First, skim a text for the gist. Then read it again more closely and focus on the details.

Tips for improving reading speed:

- Try to read groups of words, not individual words.
- Read to the end of each sentence or paragraph. Don't go back to reread words or phrases.
- Notice clues in the text such as highlighted text (**bold** words, words in *italics*, etc.). They may tell you which parts of the reading are important.
- Focus on section headings and the first and last lines of paragraphs. They can show you how the text is organized.
- Use context to guess the meaning of new words and phrases. Don't use a dictionary when you read a passage the first time.

## Thinking critically

As you read, ask yourself questions about what the writer is saying, and how and why the writer is presenting the information.

Important critical thinking skills for academic reading and writing:

- Analyzing: studying a text in close detail to identify important ideas
- Evaluating: using evidence to decide how important or useful something is
- Inferring: "reading between the lines;" in other words, identifying what a writer is saying indirectly, rather than directly
- Synthesizing: gathering and analyzing information and ideas from more than one source
- Reflecting: relating ideas and information in a text to your own personal experience and beliefs

## Note taking

Taking notes as you read will help you understand the meaning and organization of a text. Note-taking is also a way to record the most important ideas and information from a reading. You can use your notes to prepare for an exam or complete a writing assignment.

Techniques for effective note taking:

- As you read, underline or highlight important information such as dates, names, places, and other facts.
- Take notes in the margin—as you read, note the main idea and supporting details next to each paragraph. Also, note your own ideas or questions about the paragraph.
- On paper or on a computer, write the key points of the text in your own words.
- Keep your notes short—include short headings to organize the information, key words and phrases (not full sentences), and abbreviations and symbols.
- Use a graphic organizer to take notes, particularly if the reading discusses cause and effect, problem and solution, or time sequence.

### Useful abbreviations

| | | | | |
|---|---|---|---|---|
| approx. | approximately | impt | important | |
| ca. | about, around (date / year) | incl. | including | |
| cd | could | info | information | |
| Ch. | Chapter | p. (pp.) | page (pages) | |
| devt | development | para. | paragraph | |
| e.g./ex. | example | re: | regarding, concerning | |
| etc. | and others / and the rest | wd | would | |
| excl. | excluding | yr(s) | years(s) | |
| govt | government | C20 | 20th century | |

### Useful symbols

| | |
|---|---|
| → | leads to / causes |
| ↑ | increases / increased |
| ↓ | decreases / decreased |
| & or + | and |
| ∴ | therefore |
| b/c | because |
| w/ | with |
| = | is the same as |
| > | is more than |
| < | is less than |

## Learning vocabulary

You probably will not remember a new word or phrase after reading or hearing it once. You need to use the word several times. Then it will stay in your long-term memory.

Strategies for learning vocabulary:

- Use flash cards. Write the words you want to learn on one side of an index card. Write the definition and/or an example sentence that uses the word on the other side. Use your flash cards to test your knowledge of new vocabulary.
- Keep a vocabulary journal. When you come across a new word or phrase, write a short definition of the word (in English, if possible) and the sentence or situation where you found it (its context). Write another sentence of your own that uses the word. Include any common collocations. (See the Word Partners boxes in this book for examples of collocations.)

## Common affixes

Some words contain an affix at the start of the word (*prefix*) and/or at the end (*suffix*). These affixes can be useful for guessing the meaning of unfamiliar words and for expanding your vocabulary. In general, a prefix affects the meaning of a word, whereas a suffix affects its part of speech. (See the Word Link boxes in this book for specific examples.)

| Prefix | Meaning | Example |
|---|---|---|
| *con-* | together, with | connected |
| *dis-* | not | disappear |
| *im-* | not | impossible |
| *pre-* | before | predict |
| *re-* | back, again | return |
| *un-* | not | unusual |

| Suffix | Part of Speech | Example |
|---|---|---|
| *-able/-ible* | adjective | comfortable |
| *-al* | adjective | social |
| *-ance/-ence* | noun | distance, experience |
| *-ate* | verb | calculate |
| *-ed* | adjective | crowded |
| *-ent* | adjective | confident |
| *-er/-or* | noun | performer, professor |
| *-ful* | adjective | successful |
| *-ity* | noun | activity |
| *-ly* | adverb | constantly |
| *-ment* | noun | movement |
| *-tion* | noun | celebration |

# Tips for Writing

## What is a sentence?

A sentence is a group of words that expresses an idea. Sentences begin with capital letters and end with punctuation marks such as periods (.), question marks (?), and exclamation points (!). A sentence must have at least one subject and one verb. Most sentences also include other words such as adjectives (*largest*), adverbs (*constantly*), prepositions (*throughout*), and connecting words (*and*).

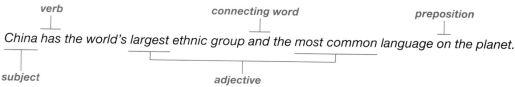

## Proofreading tips

### Capitalization

Remember to capitalize the following items:

- the first letter of the word at the beginning of every sentence
- proper names such as names of people, geographical names, company names, and names of organizations.
- days, months, and holidays
- the word *I*
- the first letter of a title such as the title of a movie or a book
- the words in titles that have meaning (content words), e.g., *Living on the Edge*. Don't capitalize *a*, *an*, *the*, *and*, or prepositions such as *to*, *for*, *of*, *from*, *at*, *in*, and *on* unless they are the first word of a title.

### Punctuation

Remember these rules:

- Use a question mark (?) at the end of every question. Use a period (.) at the end of any sentence that is not a question.
- Exclamation marks (!), which indicate strong feelings such as surprise or joy, are generally not used in academic writing.
- Use commas (,) to separate a list of three or more things. (*They travel through dangerous lands, encounter wild animals, and experience extreme situations.*)
- Use a comma before a combining word (coordinating conjunction)—*and*, *but*, *so*, *yet*, *or*, and *nor*—that joins two sentences. (*Fuentes was worried about sea turtle eggs, so she got help from local rangers.*)
- Use an apostrophe (') for showing possession. (*Only Baumgartner's special suit protected him from these dangers.*)

### Other Proofreading Tips:

- Read your sentences out loud. Use your finger or a pen to point to each word as you read it.
- Have someone else read your sentences and give comments or ask you questions.
- When your computer's spell-check suggests a correction, check it before you accept the change.
- Remember to pay attention to the following items:
  - short words such as *is*, *and*, *but*, *or*, *it*, *to*, *for*, *from*, and *so*
  - spelling of proper nouns
  - numbers and dates
- Keep a list of spelling and grammar mistakes that you commonly make so that you can be aware of them as you edit your draft.

Watch out for words that are similar:

- *there*, *their*, and *they're*
- *where*, *wear*, *we're*, and *were*
- *through* and *threw*
- *to*, *too*, and *two*
- *whose* and *who's*
- *affect* and *effect*
- *your* and *you're*
- *write* and *right*
- *by*, *buy*, and *bye*
- *quit*, *quiet*, and *quite*
- *its* and *it's*
- *then* and *than*
- *week* and *weak*

## Common signal phrases

**Giving reasons**

This is because (of) . . .
One reason (for this) is . . .
The main reason is . . .
Another reason is . . .

**Adding information**

Also, . . .
In addition, . . .
Finally, . . .

**Giving an opinion**

In my opinion, . . .
I think/feel that . . .
I believe (that) . . .

## Coordinating conjunctions

Coordinating conjunctions connect independent clauses.

| Purpose | Coordinating Conjunction | Example |
|---|---|---|
| to add information | and | I post on Facebook once a day, and I post on Pinterest once a week. |
| to show contrast | but | I never post on Pinterest, but I post a lot on Twitter. |
| to give a choice | or | I can send the photo by email, or I can post it on Facebook. |
| to show result | so | Climate change is melting Arctic ice, so the polar bears' habitat is disappearing. |

## Grammar Reference

## Unit 1

**Language for Writing:** Simple Present Tense of *Be* and Other Verbs

**Affirmative Statements with *Be***

| Subject | Am / Are / Is | Noun, Adjective, Prepositional Phrase |
|---|---|---|
| I | am | a student. <br> excited. <br> at work. |
| You <br> We <br> They | are | a student. / students. <br> late. <br> at home. |
| He <br> She | is | a student. <br> tired. <br> fun. |
| It | | a website. <br> great. <br> on the table. |

**Affirmative Statements with Other Verbs**

| Subject | Verb | Spelling Rules |
|---|---|---|
| I | **like** Pinterest. <br> **have** a laptop. <br> **study** in the evenings. | Use the base form of a verb with *I*, *you*, *we*, and *they*. For most verbs, use the base form + *-s* with *he*, *she*, and *it*. |
| You <br> We <br> They | **use** Facebook. <br> **live** on Main Street. <br> **study** in the library. | |
| He <br> She | **loves** Tagged. <br> **has** a tablet. <br> **studies** after class. | Some verbs are irregular. You do not use the base form + *-s* with *he*, *she*, and *it*. <br> **do—does**   **have—has**   **go—goes** |
| It | **looks** great | If a verb ends in *-y*, drop the *-y* and add *-ies*. |

## Unit 2

**Language for Writing:** Simple Present Negative of *Be* and Other Verbs

| Negative Statement with *Be* | | |
|---|---|---|
| **Subject** | **Am / Are / Is** | |
| I | **am not** | bored. |
| You (singular or plural) We They | **are not** **aren't** | nervous. |
| He She It | **is not** **isn't** | alone. at work. |

| Negative Statements: Other Verbs | | |
|---|---|---|
| **Subject** | **Do / Does not** | |
| I You We They | **do not** **don't** | take risks. |
| He She It | **does not** **doesn't** | |

## Unit 3

**Language for Writing:** Comparative Forms of Adjectives and Nouns

| Comparative Adjectives | | |
|---|---|---|
| With one-syllable adjectives, add *-er*. Add *-r* if the adjective ends in *-e*. | | |
| **Adjective** | **Comparative form** | **Example** |
| fast | faster | The subway is **faster** than the bus. |
| nice | nicer | The train is **nicer** than the subway. |

| | | |
|---|---|---|
| With two-syllable adjectives ending in *-y*, drop the *-y* and add *-ier*. | | |
| **Adjective** | **Comparative form** | **Example** |
| busy | busier | New York is **busier** than San Francisco. |
| dirty | dirtier | The bus is **dirtier** than the subway. |

| | | |
|---|---|---|
| With most other two-syllable adjectives and adjectives with three or more syllables, use *more*. | | |
| **Adjective** | **Comparative form** | **Example** |
| crowded | more crowded | The train is **more crowded** than the subway. |
| expensive | more expensive | The train is **more expensive** than the subway. |

## Unit 7

**Language for Writing:** Simple Past of *Be* and Other Verbs

### Simple Past of *Be*

| Subject | Was / Were | Noun, Adjective, Prepositional Phrase |
|---|---|---|
| I | **was** | a nurse. <br> late. <br> at work. |
| You (singular or plural) <br> We <br> They | **were** | a teacher. / teachers. <br> excited. <br> in class. |
| He <br> She | **was** | an inventor. <br> talented. <br> in London. |
| It | | a new invention. <br> exciting. <br> on the news. |

### Simple Past of Other Verbs

| Subject | Verb | Spelling Rules |
|---|---|---|
| I <br><br> You <br> We <br> They <br><br> He <br> She <br><br> It | **invented** something. <br><br> **lived** in New York. <br><br> **met** a famous inventor. <br><br> **grew** up in a small town. | Add *-ed* to the base form of a regular verb to form the simple past. Add *-d* if the verb already ends in *-e*. <br> **invent—invented**   **live—lived** <br><br> For verbs that end in consonant + *-y*, drop the *-y* and add *-ied*. <br> **study—studied** <br><br> For most verbs that end in consonant + vowel + consonant, double the final consonant and add *-ed*. <br> **stop-stopped** |

### Some verbs have irregular past forms.

| | | |
|---|---|---|
| become—became | find—found | put—put |
| begin—began | forget—forgot | read—read |
| build—built | get—got | say—said |
| buy—bought | give—gave | see—saw |
| come—came | go—went | spend—spent |
| do—did | have—had | take—took |
| draw—drew | hear—heard | teach—taught |
| eat—ate | know—knew | think—thought |
| grow up—grew up | make—made | understand—understood |
| fall—fell | meet—met | write—wrote |

## Vocabulary Index

*These words are on the Academic Word List (AWL). The AWL is a list of the 570 most frequent word families in academic texts. The list does not include words that are among the most frequent 2,000 words of English. For more information on the AWL, see http://www.victoria. ac.nz/lals/resources/ academicwordlist/.

# Acknowledgments

The authors and publisher would like to thank the following reviewers for their help during the development of this series:

## UNITED STATES AND CANADA

Gokhan Alkanat, Auburn University at Montgomery, AL; Nikki Ashcraft, Shenandoah University, VA; Karin Avila-John, University of Dayton, OH; John Baker, Oakland Community College, MI; Shirley Baker, Alliant International University, CA; Michelle Bell, University of South Florida, FL; Nancy Boyer, Golden West College, CA; Kathy Brenner, BU/CELOP, Mattapan, MA; Janna Brink, Mt. San Antonio College, Chino Hills, CA; Carol Brutza, Gateway Community College, CT; Sarah Camp, University of Kentucky, Center for ESL, KY; Maria Caratini, Eastfield College, TX; Ana Maria Cepero, Miami Dade College, Miami, FL; Daniel Chaboya, Tulsa Community College, OK; Patricia Chukwueke, English Language Institute – UCSD Extension, CA; Julia A. Correia, Henderson State University, CT; Suzanne Crisci, Bunker Hill Community College, MA; Lina Crocker, University of Kentucky, Lexington, KY; Katie Crowder, University of North Texas, TX; Joe Cunningham, Park University, Kansas City, MO; Lynda Dalgish, Concordia College, NY; Jeffrey Diluglio, Center for English Language and Orientation Programs: Boston University, MA; Scott Dirks, Kaplan International Center at Harvard Square, MA; Kathleen Dixon, SUNY Stony Brook - Intensive English Center, Stony Brook, NY; Margo Downey, Boston University, Boston, MA; John Drezek, Richland College, TX; Qian Du, Ohio State University, Columbus, OH; Leslie Kosel Eckstein, Hillsborough Community College, FL; Anwar El-Issa, Antelope Valley College, CA; Beth Kozbial Ernst, University of Wisconsin-Eau Claire, WI; Anrisa Fannin, The International Education Center at Diablo Valley College, CA; Jennie Farnell, Greenwich Japanese School, Greenwich, CT; Rosa Vasquez Fernandez, John F. Kennedy Institute Of Languages, Inc., Boston, MA; Mark Fisher, Lone Star College, TX; Celeste Flowers, University of Central Arkansas, AR; John Fox, English Language Institute, GA; Pradel R. Frank, Miami Dade College, FL; Sherri Fujita, Hawaii Community College, Hilo, HI; Sally Gearheart, Santa Rosa Jr. College, CA; Elizabeth Gillstrom, The University of Pennsylvania, Philadelphia, PA; Sheila Goldstein, Rockland Community College, Brentwood, NY; Karen Grubbs, ELS Language Centers, FL; Sudeepa Gulati, Long Beach City College, Torrance, CA; Joni Hagigeorges, Salem State University, MA; Marcia Peoples Halio, English Language Institute, University of Delaware, DE; Kara Hanson, Oregon State University, Corvallis, OR; Suha Hattab, Triton College, Chicago, IL; Marla Heath, Sacred Heart Univiversity and Norwalk Community College, Stamford, CT; Valerie Heming, University of Central Missouri, MO; Mary Hill, North Shore Community College, MA; Harry Holden, North Lake College, Dallas, TX; Ingrid Holm, University of Massachusetts Amherst, MA; Katie Hurter, Lone Star College – North Harris, TX; Barbara Inerfeld, Program in American Language Studies (PALS) Rutgers University/New Brunswick, Piscataway, NJ; Justin Jernigan, Georgia Gwinnett College, GA; Barbara Jonckheere, ALI/CSULB, Long Beach, CA; Susan Jordan, Fisher College, MA; Maria Kasparova, Bergen Community College, NJ; Maureen Kelbert, Vancouver Community College, Surrey, BC, Canada; Gail Kellersberger, University of Houston-Downtown, TX; David Kent, Troy University, Goshen, AL; Daryl Kinney, Los Angeles City College, CA; Jennifer Lacroix, Center for English Language and Orientation Programs: Boston University, MA; Stuart Landers, Missouri State University, Springfield, MO; Mary Jo Fletcher LaRocco, Ph.D., Salve Regina University, Newport, RI; Bea Lawn, Gavilan College, Gilroy, CA; Margaret V. Layton, University of Nevada, Reno Intensive English Language Center, NV; Alice Lee, Richland College, Mesquite, TX; Heidi Lieb, Bergen Community College, NJ; Kerry Linder, Language Studies International New York, NY; Jenifer Lucas-Uygun, Passaic County Community College, Paterson, NJ; Alison MacAdams, Approach International Student Center, MA; Julia MacDonald, Brock University, Saint Catharines, ON, Canada; Craig Machado, Norwalk Community College, CT; Andrew J. MacNeill, Southwestern College, CA; Melanie A. Majeski, Naugatuck Valley Community College, CT; Wendy Maloney, College of DuPage, Aurora, IL; Chris Mares, University of Maine – Intensive English Institute, Maine; Josefina Mark, Union County College, NJ; Connie Mathews, Nashville State Community College, TN; Bette Matthews, Mid-Pacific Institute, HI; Richard McDorman, inlingua Language Centers (Miami, FL) and Pennsylvania State University, Pompano Beach, FL; Sara McKinnon, College of Marin, CA; Christine Mekkaoui, Pittsburg State University, KS; Holly A. Milkowart, Johnson County Community College, KS; Donna Moore, Hawaii Community College, Hilo, HI; Ruth W. Moore, International English Center, University of Colorado at Boulder, CO; Kimberly McGrath Moreira, University of Miami, FL; Warren Mosher, University of Miami, FL; Sarah Moyer, California State University Long Beach, CA; Lukas Murphy, Westchester Community College, NY; Elena Nehrebecki, Hudson Community College, NJ; Bjarne Nielsen, Central Piedmont Community College, North Carolina; David Nippoldt, Reedley College, CA; Nancy Nystrom, University Of Texas At San Antonio, Austin, TX; Jane O'Connor, Emory College, Atlanta, GA; Daniel E. Opacki, SIT Graduate Institute, Brattleboro, VT; Lucia Parsley, Virginia Commonwealth University, VA; Wendy Patriquin, Parkland College, IL; Nancy Pendleton, Cape Cod Community College, Attleboro, MA; Marion Piccolomini, Communicate With Ease, LTD, PA; Barbara Pijan, Portland State University, Portland, OR; Marjorie Pitts, Ohio Northern University, Ada, OH; Carolyn Prager, Spanish-American Institute, NY; Eileen Prince, Prince Language Associates Incorporated, MA; Sema Pulak, Texas A & M University, TX; Mary Kay Purcell, University of Evansville, Evansville, IN; Christina Quartararo, St. John's University, Jamaica, NY; James T. Raby, Clark University, MA; Anouchka Rachelson, Miami-Dade College, FL; Sherry Rasmussen, DePaul University, IL; Amy Renehan, University of Washington, WA; Daniel Rivas, Irvine Valley College, Irvine, CA; Esther Robbins, Prince George's Community College, PA; Bruce Rogers, Spring International Language Center at Arapahoe College, Littleton, CO; Helen Roland, Miami Dade College, FL; Linda Roth, Vanderbilt University English Language Center, TN; Janine Rudnick, El Paso Community College, TX; Paula Sanchez, Miami Dade College – Kendall Campus, FL; Deborah Sandstrom, Tutorium in Intensive English at University of Illinois at Chicago, Elmhurst, IL; Marianne Hsu Santelli, Middlesex County College, NJ; Elena Sapp, INTO Oregon State University, Corvallis, OR; Alice Savage, Lone Star College System: North Harris, TX; Jitana Schaefer, Pensacola State College, Pensacola, FL; Lynn Ramage Schaefer, University of Central Arkansas, AR; Ann Schroth, Johnson & Wales University, Dayville, CT; Margaret Shippey, Miami Dade College, FL; Lisa Sieg, Murray State University, KY; Samanthia Slaight, North Lake College, Richardson, TX;

Ann Snider, UNK University of NE Kearney, Kearney, NE; Alison Stamps, ESL Center at Mississippi State University, Mississippi; Peggy Street, ELS Language Centers, Miami, FL; Lydia Streiter, York College Adult Learning Center, NY; Steve Strizver, Miami Beach, FL; Nicholas Taggart, Arkansas State University, AR; Marcia Takacs, Coastline Community College, CA; Tamara Teffeteller, University of California Los Angeles, American Language Center, CA; Adrianne Aiko Thompson, Miami Dade College, Miami, FL; Rebecca Toner, English Language Programs, University of Pennsylvania, PA; Evina Baquiran Torres, Zoni Language Centers, NY; William G. Trudeau, Missouri Southern State University, MO; Troy Tucker, Edison State College, FL; Maria Vargas-O'Neel, Miami Dade College, FL; America Vazquez, Miami Dade College, FL; Alison Vinande, Modesto Junior College, CA; Christie Ward, IELP, Central CT State University, Hartford, CT; Colin Ward, Lone Star College - North Harris, Houston, TX; Denise Warner, Lansing Community College, Lansing, MI; Rita Rutkowski Weber, University of Wisconsin – Milwaukee, WI; James Wilson, Cosumnes River College, Sacramento, CA; Dolores "Lorrie" Winter, California State University Fullerton, Buena Park, CA; Wendy Wish-Bogue, Valencia Community College, FL; Cissy Wong, Sacramento City College, CA; Sarah Worthington, Tucson, Arizona; Kimberly Yoder, Kent State University, ESL Center, OH.

## ASIA

Nor Azni Abdullah, Universiti Teknologi Mara; Morgan Bapst, Seoul National University of Science and Technology; Herman Bartelen, Kanda Institute of Foreign Languages, Sano; Maiko Berger, Ritsumeikan Asia Pacific University; Thomas E. Bieri, Nagoya College; Paul Bournhonesque, Seoul National University of Technology; Joyce Cheah Kim Sim, Taylor's University, Selangor Darul Ehsan; Michael C. Cheng, National Chengchi University; Fu-Dong Chiou, National Taiwan University; Derek Currie, Korea University, Sejong Institute of Foreign Language Studies; Wendy Gough, St. Mary College/Nunoike Gaigo Senmon Gakko, Ichinomiya; Christoph A. Hafner, City University of Hong Kong; Monica Hamciuc, Ritsumeikan Asia-Pacific University, Kagoshima; Rob Higgens, Ritsumeikan University; Wenhua Hsu, I-Shou University; Lawrie Hunter, Kochi University of Technology; Helen Huntley, Hanoi University; Debra Jones, Tokyo Woman's Christian University, Tokyo; Shih Fan Kao, JinWen University of Science and Technology; Ikuko Kashiwabara, Osaka Electro-Communication University; Alyssa Kim, Hankuk University of Foreign Studies; Richard S. Lavin, Prefecturla University of Kumamoto; Mike Lay, American Institute Cambodia; Byoung-Kyo Lee, Yonsei University; Lin Li, Capital Normal University, Beijing; Bien Thi Thanh Mai, The International University – Vietnam National University, Ho Chi Minh City; Hudson Murrell, Baiko Gakuin University; Keiichi Narita, Niigata University; Orapin Nasawang, Udon Thani Rajabhat University; Huynh Thi Ai Nguyen, Vietnam USA Society; James Pham, IDP Phnom Penh; John Racine, Dokkyo University; Duncan Rose, British Council Singapore; Greg Rouault, Konan University, Hirao School of Management, Osaka; Simone Samuels, The Indonesia Australia Language Foundation, Jakarta; Yuko Shimizu, Ritsumeikan University; Wang Songmei, Beijing Institute of Education Faculty; Richmond Stroupe, Soka University; Peechaya Suriyawong, Udon Thani Rajabhat University; Teoh Swee Ai, Universiti Teknologi Mara; Chien-Wen Jenny Tseng, National Sun Yat-Sen University; Hajime Uematsu, Hirosaki University; Sy Vanna, Newton Thilay School, Phnom Penh; Matthew Watterson, Hongik University; Anthony Zak, English Language Center, Shantou University.

## LATIN AMERICA AND THE CARIBBEAN

Ramon Aguilar, Universidad Tecnológica de Hermosillo, México; Lívia de Araújo Donnini Rodrigues, University of São Paolo, Brazil; Cecilia Avila, Universidad de Xapala, México; Beth Bartlett, Centro Cultural Colombo Americano, Cali, Colombia; Raúl Billini, Colegio Loyola, Dominican Republic; Nohora Edith Bryan, Universidad de La Sabana, Colombia; Raquel Hernández Cantú, Instituto Tecnológico de Monterrey, Mexico; Millie Commander, Inter American University of Puerto Rico, Puerto Rico; José Alonso Gaxiola Soto, CEI Universidad Autonoma de Sinaloa, Mazatlán, Mexico; Raquel Hernandez, Tecnologico de Monterrey, Mexico; Edwin Marín-Arroyo, Instituto Tecnológico de Costa Rica; Rosario Mena, Instituto Cultural Dominico-Americano, Dominican Republic; Elizabeth Ortiz Lozada, COPEI-COPOL English Institute, Ecuador; Gilberto Rios Zamora, Sinaloa State Language Center, Mexico; Patricia Veciños, El Instituto Cultural Argentino Norteamericano, Argentina; Isabela Villas Boas, Casa Thomas Jefferson, Brasília, Brazil; Roxana Viñes, Language Two School of English, Argentina.

## EUROPE, MIDDLE EAST, AND NORTH AFRICA

Tom Farkas, American University of Cairo, Egypt; Ghada Hozayen, Arab Academy for Science, Technology and Maritime Transport, Egypt; Tamara Jones, ESL Instructor, SHAPE Language Center, Belgium; Jodi Lefort, Sultan Qaboos University, Oman; Neil McBeath, Sultan Qaboos University, Oman; Barbara R. Reimer, CERTESL, UAE University, UAE; Nashwa Nashaat Sobhy, The American University in Cairo, Egypt; Virginia Van Hest-Bastaki, Kuwait University, Kuwait.

## AUSTRALIA

Susan Austin, University of South Australia, Joanne Cummins, Swinburne College; Pamela Humphreys, Griffith University.

Special thanks to Emily Ainsworth, Mark Bezodis, Mariana Fuentes, Barrington Irving, Prof. Stan Z. Li, Albert Lin, Kira Salak, Joel Sartore, and Susan Wynn for their kind assistance during this book's development.

This series is dedicated to Kristin L. Johannsen, whose love for the world's cultures and concern for the world's environment were an inspiration to family, friends, students, and colleagues.

## Critical Thinking

Analyzing 26, 44, 50, 62, 97, 117, 124, 142

Applying 62, 98, 136

Evaluating 50, 79, 86

Guessing meaning from context 7, 8, 14, 26, 44, 61, 79, 142

Making inferences 61, 68, 135

Personalizing/Reflecting 3, 7, 21, 26, 32, 37, 55, 56, 73, 74, 79, 91, 92, 111, 113, 129, 130

Predicting 4, 11, 23, 29, 41, 45, 47, 58, 65, 76, 81, 83, 94, 101, 121, 137, 139

Speculating 109

Synthesizing 9, 27, 32, 45, 50, 63, 68, 81, 86, 99, 106, 119, 124, 137, 142

## Language for Writing

Adverbs of frequency 35

Comparatives 51

Coordinating conjunctions *and*, *but*, and *or* 88–89

Giving reasons 107

Infinitives of purpose 87

Introducing your opinions 143

*Should* 144

Simple past tense 125

Simple past tense of *be* 127

Simple present tense of *be* 16

Simple present negative of *be* and other verbs 33

Simple present tense of other verbs 17

Speculating about the future 109

Using *because* 52

Using *plan*, *want*, and *hope* 69

Using time expressions 70

## Reading Skills

Identifying purpose 8

Previewing 23, 41

Scanning for key details 80

Understanding main ideas and supporting ideas of paragraphs 62

Taking notes 136

Understanding pronoun reference 118

Understanding reasons 98

## Visual Literacy

Interpreting graphic information:

- graphs/charts 12, 13, 38, 39, 48, 56

- infographics 2, 12, 13, 49, 60, 131

- labeled image 116

- maps 49, 75, 78

Using graphic organizers:

- concept maps 50, 97

- outlines and T-charts 44, 128, 135, 136, 142, 145, 146

- flow charts 97, 117

- Venn diagrams 86, 106

## Vocabulary Skills

Building vocabulary 4, 10, 22, 28, 40, 46, 58, 64, 76, 82, 94, 100, 114, 120, 132, 138

Using vocabulary 4, 11, 22, 28, 40, 47, 58, 65, 76, 94, 114, 121, 132, 139

Expanding vocabulary 11, 28, 47, 65, 83, 101, 121, 139

Understanding word parts 4, 10, 47, 65, 76, 83, 114, 132

Understanding collocations 4, 11, 22, 40, 46, 58, 82, 94, 120, 121, 132, 138

Understanding word usage 4, 28, 64, 101, 139